Roof
Slates
and
Other
Poems
of
Pierre
Reverdy

Pablo Picasso. "Portrait de Reverdy," © SPADEM, Paris/VAGA, New York, 1981 (courtesy of the Bibliothèque Littéraire Jacques Doucet).

Roof
Slates
and
Other
Poems
of
Pierre
Reverdy

Pierre Reverdy

translated, with prefaces by
Mary Ann Caws
and
Patricia Terry

Northeastern University Press
Boston 1981

Editors: *Norma Fryatt, Judith Brudnick*
Production editor: *Deborah Kops*
Designer: *Catherine Dorin*
Jacket design: *Catherine Dorin*

Reverdy, Pierre, 1899–1960.
   Roof slates and other poems of Pierre Reverdy.

   Bibliography: p.
   I. Caws, Mary Ann.   II. Terry, Patricia Ann,
1929–   III. Title.
PQ2635.E85A17   1981   841'.912   80-26806
ISBN 0-930350-09-X

Printed in the United States of America

When one refuses the temptations of an elsewhere, the illusions of a beyond, the mirages of a future. And when one stands on the earth, as near as possible to things, listening to oneself, with one's eyes open, stubbornly. And when, across from you, reality at its fullest repulses you like a smooth wall with no escape. Imprisons you and exiles you. Or when the single window under the eaves, the skylight of the garret, holds you captive and isolated from a world in splinters and slipping away, whose discordant particles slide endlessly over an ill-lit slope. And when even the solidity of the wall that you seem to run into and which your head could at least be shattered by, is only a fog lifting. And forming again, opening, for the time of a poem, onto the debris of a life dispersed. . . . The poet has nothing to say. "He has nothing to give except what he has not." Nothing but this. Neither impoverishing nor enriching. Nothing else, but with a monotonous obstinacy, a desperate bitterness. Saying nothing, in the closest proximity and with the simplest words, saying nothing but the thing of each instant, finally given wings. . . . The daily bread, the daily nothingness. A priceless poverty. Which gnaws dully at the heart and fortifies hunger like some reason for being and for enduring, — the touchstone of a poetics. . . . Wind, or emptiness, or nothing. . . . An ardent poverty, froth of solitude, essence of single tone. The poet, that is, no one, before the wall which arrests us and which he traverses, continues to write on the sand and the dust. . . . The less he has to give the more he gives. He keeps space open.

And the sun begins a perilous ascent.

Jacques Dupin, "The Difficulty of the Sun: Concerning Pierre Reverdy," in *A la Rencontre de Pierre Reverdy* (Fondation Maeght, 1970).

(translated by Mary Ann Caws)

Table of Contents

Preface

We chose the texts with two criteria in mind — that they represent Reverdy at his finest, and at the same time read as poems in English. Pierre Reverdy's *Les Ardoises du toit* (The Roof Slates), representing the finest poems in verse, is given completely, and is followed by a chronological selection of prose poems, ranging over almost half a century, from 1915 to 1959. Thus the reader has examples of two aspects in this poet of the "static" text, whose importance has perhaps not been sufficiently stressed, and whose oddly appealing poetic character can best be judged after these two different sorts of poetic expression have been juxtaposed. If the verse poems, in their layout and their very nature, resemble the poems of no one else, no more do the prose poems fit into any simple scheme of differentiation between "prose" and "verse." The beginning of "Corridor" offers a convenient if fortuitous entrance to both, and to certain problems of their translation:

> There are two of us
>> On the same line where everything follows
>> In night's winding ways

"Two of us" may refer to the poet and a companion, to the poet and his reader, to the poet's own duality, or the reader's. "Everything follows" (tout se suit) indicates an unbroken order, as in "one day follows another," or, in its more literally reflexive sense, suggests that everything is in its own order, and that a beginning may be preceded by an ending. The relationship of these various meanings to the "winding ways" either places "the two of us" within the unpredictable mazes of the night, or emphasizes rather a contrast of "lines" with the order of the poem itself predominating. The latter reading will be characteristic of the verse poems, while those in prose tend more to dramatize the poet's difficult experience of darkness. In both orientations the absence of convenient reflexives in English is a serious problem in translating a poet whose constant use of reflexive verbs is symptomatic of introspection in himself and self-awareness in his poems.

In the mobile-like construction of the verse poems the reader's "way" can be complex indeed, involving many reversals in which endings will be seen as beginnings. The prose poems are more direct. Whether narrative or descriptive they are poems by virtue of their brevity, the musical quality of the phrases, the density of their language, and their rejection of all that is merely anecdotal in favor of a subjective and dramatic coherence. What is presented is often enigmatic or ambiguous, always extraordinary. In the verse poems, particularly those of *Les Ardoises du toit*, the elements of the poem may be commonplace in themselves; they function aesthetically in juxtaposition.

If we look at a prose poem containing themes that recur in verse, this essential difference will be apparent. In "Strokes and Figures," from a collection published three years before *Les Ardoises du toit*, the world of nature is seen to differ from the urban by its combination of color, light, and clarity, the last two expressed by *éclaircie*, a clearing in the sky, and *clairière*, a clearing in the forest. The imprisoning linear framework of the city has another kind of clarity, that of colorless geometric forms, lines in the service of *bâtisses humaines*, buildings where people live in ugliness. A third domain, the mind of the poet, contains, like the city, "nothing but lines," lines that the poet seeks to "put in order." The poem, however, has a linear order of its own: the clear outline of a formless dilemma.

The opposition between a clearing in nature and clarity in the mind occurs also in "Patience" from *Les Ardoises du toit*. The paratactic structure of the poem, its greater number of elements, and much rarer indications of opinion or emotion, make its "nothing is clear inside my head" very different from the corresponding statement in "Strokes and Figures." One has an impression of what the lack of clarity is in itself, other than simply the contrary of order. In "Patience" the connection between nature and the poet's mind is made through echoes and repetitions. The "clearing" and "nothing is clear" are related by identical sound and opposed meaning; in "Strokes and Figures" color, line, and a lack of order are related by semantic contrast alone.

The discourse in "Strokes and Figures" concerns itself with lines and geometric forms; in "False Portal or Portrait" verbal expression becomes directly spatial: "In this unmoving square," "in the middle," "Tears are rolling through this space." Shapes are also part of the poem's own structure:

> In this unmoving square
> Inside four lines
>   A space for the play of white

as opposed to "in the city . . . the square of the windows." Shapes may materialize through suggestion: the curve of "your cheek," hinting at the roundness of the moon (*lune* to be read also as *l'une*, the one), and anticipating, phonetically and by the transfer of light, the subsequent illumination, *s'allume*.

"Strokes [*traits*] and Figures" is the subject; "False Portal" is a "Porte/Trait," a preliminary experience of the poem. The lines surround a mirror that offers a perspective illuminated, not by moonlight, but by the poet ("I am the lamp to guide me"). The mirror-image is both a true representation and a false one, being, as Reverdy might have said, *à l'envers*, in the wrong direction, in reverse, or inside out — all of which are ways of reading the poem. Had the mirror appeared in a prose poem it might well have represented for the reader simply an element of the description or narration. From the reader's side of the false portal, he must perceive the poem as mirroring itself, its portrait, as well as his reading. The mirror is also the mediation between dramatic space and page as well as between poet and reader. The face contemplated thus reveals itself as another face of the text, as the page incorporates all possible reflections.

To this mirror of a poem, the I ("I am the lamp . . . ") and the eye serve as guides. The fact that an eye with a finger on its lid is probably closed indicates the interiority of the vision, a point reinforced by the rhyme *guide/humide*. The door's falsity, an obstacle to progress beyond itself, is thus an opening in another direction.

Mary Ann Caws and *Patricia Terry*

We should like to thank, most warmly,
François Chapon, Jacques Dupin, Étienne-Alain Hubert,
and the Comité Reverdy for their help
and their encouragement.

Grateful acknowledgment is made to the following for permission to reprint from the copyrighted works of Pierre Reverdy: to Flammarion for excerpts from *La Plupart du Temps*, © Librairie Ernest Flammarion, 1967 and to Mercure de France for excerpts from *Main d'Oeuvre*, © Mercure de France, 1949.

M. A. C.
P. T.

Introduction

Symbolist and post-Symbolist French poets have wished to free poetry from whatever they defined as "literature." Verlaine wanted poetry to be "music" as opposed to "eloquence." Rimbaud, far more ambitious, believed that poetry could transform life itself by detaching the things of this world from their environment of habit and custom. The Surrealists, not content with Rimbaud's program of "systematic dis-ordering of the senses," tried to eliminate conscious reaction to experience altogether. The result would be an art dictated by the subconscious, and thus independent of craftsmanship. Apollinaire, a beacon, as Reverdy said, for contemporary poets, gave the Surrealists their name but did not join them in reducing, or, as they saw it, exalting the poet to his undifferentiated subconscious. His own poetry introduced a new freedom of vocabulary and the beginnings of nonsequential presentation of the elements of the poem, a primary technique being the elimination of punctuation.

Compared to these predecessors, Reverdy strikes one as simultaneously more austere and more violent. Where Apollinaire, even at his most unorthodox, still used his own emotions as the materials of his poems, Reverdy allows himself to be apparent, if at all, only as an abstract presence, the mind that both orders and inhabits the still life or the landscape. Very much in the manner of the Cubist painters who were his friends, Reverdy exists in his works as a diffuse intensity by his very refusal of a perspective that would dictate the way in which the elements of the poem or painting are to be perceived. The particular elements Reverdy chose were often the same modest, everyday objects found in the paintings of Braque, Picasso, and Gris: window and table, pipe and playing cards, guitar and newspaper, lamp and wine bottle. These objects occur simultaneously on the undisguised two-dimensional surface of the paintings. In the poems they are juxtaposed in such a way that although they must, by the nature of the process of reading, be perceived one after another, their position on the page, syntactical ambiguities, and the absence of connecting particles force the eye and the mind to grasp them all at once. It is in this sense that Reverdy wanted to make a "static poem" which would resemble a painting.

Born and educated in Toulouse and Narbonne, Reverdy moved to Paris in 1910 to live the rest of his life there and in the equally gray climate of the Abbaye de Solesme. But he seems never to have lost a nostalgia for the more brilliant landscapes of his youth, and defined, as the aim of his art, "to oppose to the ebb and flow of emotion the moving brilliance of the earth's surface, hard, clear and dry, in the bracing air of the heights." The essay, "Note Eternelle du Présent" (1933), adds that art steals from its contact with the earth the means by which it rises ever closer to the sun.

The son and grandson of sculptors, Reverdy made of his own intangible medium something as physical as possible. On a practical level, he earned his living as a typesetter, work to which he devoted himself with a patience and a skill that can be seen in his 1918 edition of *Les Ardoises du toit*, an achievement which can be reproduced today only photographically. He had an intense appreciation of craftsmanship in all forms: hence the mutual attraction between him and Coco Chanel. Language was to be kneaded like a kind of dough in order to produce a poetry that would "glorify matter and restore it to a place of honor." As Mallarmé aspired to achieve in language something with which to confront the silent purity of the Ideal, Reverdy's no less paradoxical project was to use language as an instrument with which to construct, out of the "splendid health" of nature, a durable, and anti-natural object. This he perceived as the aim, not only of poetry, but of the arts of his time in general, and the response of painters is indicated by the affinity they obviously felt for his work.

Reverdy's poems were illustrated by the painters already mentioned, and by Matisse, Derain, La Fresnaye, and Chagall. Modigliani and Picasso, among many others, painted his portrait, and Gris' "Still Life with a Poem" is an homage to him, as is Breton's celebrated poem "Tournesol" or "Sunflower."

In 1917 Reverdy was the director of the influential journal *Nord-Sud*, and he contributed to the "Now-ist" or "Presentist" journal *Sic*, directed by Pierre-Albert Birot (1917–1918); to the early Surrealist production *Littérature*, directed by Aragon, Breton, and Philippe Soupault (1919); and later to their *Révolution surréaliste* (1925). He was responsible for the first formulation of what Breton took as his own theory of the image: "The image is a pure creation of the mind. It cannot be born from a comparison, but only by bringing together two distant objects. The greater the distance between the objects and the more appropriate, the stronger the image, the more powerful its emotional force and poetic reality" (*Nord-Sud*, no. 13, March 1918). Through his influence on such Surrealist poets as Breton and Eluard, and also directly, Reverdy's work has had a great impact on the American Imagist poets of the middle part of this century. In him can be found both ellipsis and intensity, both informality and care for new forms — in particular, the brief paratactic structures and the prose poems translated here.

Reverdy, finally, is the "plastic" poet he chose to be: at once static and quietly dynamic. Poems, he said, should be "crystals precipitated from the effervescent contact of the mind and reality." The resulting crystals are neither dark nor brilliant, but rather quietly luminous, not just in the texts themselves, but in their lasting effect. This poetry takes place indeed within a closed space: doors pulled shut, a house not to be entered, a wall blocking off exit, barriers of all sorts — but the smallest detail may lead to a wide interior space, the one we have tried to depict within our translations. Like those two objects from distant realms that constitute the powerful image, this illumination and this simultaneity may encounter each other, may interpenetrate, as they open in and out.

Chronology

1927	*Le Gant de crin*
1928	*La Balle au bond*
1929	*Sources du vent* (1925–29)
	Flaques de verre (collected prose poems)
1930	*Risques et périls* (collected short stories, 1915–28)
1937	*Ferraille*
1945	*Plupart du temps* (1915–22)
1948	*Le Livre de mon bord* (critical writings, 1930–36)
1949	*Main d'Oeuvre* (collected poems, 1913–49)
1956	*En vrac* (critical writings)
1960	Reverdy dies at Solesmes

Posthumous publications:

Note éternelle du présent, writings about art, 1923–60, ed. Étienne-Alain Hubert.

Cette émotion appelée poésie, writings about poetry, 1932–60, ed. Étienne-Alain Hubert.

Nord-Sud, Self defence and other critical writings, 1917–26, ed. Étienne-Alain Hubert.

Bibliographie des écrits de Pierre Reverdy, Étienne-Alain Hubert.

Roof
Slates
and
Other
Poems
of
Pierre
Reverdy

Les Ardoises du toit

The Roof Slates

translated by
Patricia Terry

The gaiety of language is our seigneur.
— Wallace Stevens

Although Reverdy specifically rejected the idea of Cubist poetry, the poems of *Les Ardoises du toit* are analogous to Cubist paintings. Words are treated as Juan Gris or Braque used objects, meticulously detached from identifiable contexts so that their abstract qualities, the shapes of things, the evocative energies of language, could be made to participate in a new and coherent structure. The poems in this book do not represent reality; they present themselves in its place. The movement toward a liberating abstraction began, as Reverdy reminded his contemporaries, not with the painters but with Mallarmé and with Rimbaud who was, for the young Reverdy, trying to cross the threshold between experience and art, "the first ray of light under the door."[1]

The theme of illumination is constant in *Les Ardoises du toit:* "I am the lamp to guide me," "A quick light/Gleams/It's another glow just now/that guides me," "But the lamp has just gone out," "The lantern of the departing train"; and Reverdy in his critical works emphasizes it also in connection with the reader. Reverdy's poems require an unusual amount of collaboration; they are "dark rooms" in which the only light will come from the reader's mind.[2] Reverdy believed that the critic might provide additional light, not by analyzing the human experience in which the poem has its source, as if the poem itself had been useless, but by showing how that experience, unsatisfying, even terrible in itself, becomes positive and sometimes exalting in the poem. Thematic accounts make of Reverdy's work an unrelieved expression of hopelessness, while for its author the purpose of art was not to increase human suffering, but to provide a means of escape from it. The artist, by the strength of his aesthetic transformations of the real, reaches a higher domain where he can "breathe and live." His works mark out a route that others need only follow to this freedom.[3]

Metaphor is the primary instrument used to extract from reality what is *not there*, and thus not bound by the subordination of mind to matter. Two apparently unrelated things are brought together in a new unity whose authenticity is guaranteed by the emotion it evokes: "the surprise and the joy of finding oneself in the presence of something new."[4] In Reverdy's poems the comparative aspect that persists in classical metaphor is greatly attenuated, and the creative function of language itself brought into higher relief.

A phrase like "the empty bell" ("Secret"), isolated within a poem, is a cluster of meanings (silence made physical, loss of a music that had been a communication, unexplained deterioration) which evoke the other pole of the metaphor, a cluster of responses (a sense of loss, an awareness of silence as a positive, uneasiness) including the aesthetic component which is delight at what language accomplishes with such efficiency. The metaphor then has an influence on, and is itself affected by, others in the poem. In "Secret" "the empty bell" is immediately followed by "the dead birds," placed directly below so that it seems a synonym and adds an intensified fear to the silence. The time is "nine o'clock," but in this context, the reverse of "Sound of a Bell," time would already be uncounted. The only sounds in the poem are human: what may have been a sigh, and a man singing. He is in the open air, and in a large empty space on the page, but being also "in front of the door" he must be close to the window which, in the following line, opens "without a sound."

The individual elements composing a poem are often prompted by obsessions the reader may not share with Reverdy, but they are impersonal and ambiguous enough to serve as images for more generalized anxieties. "The ground was full of holes," "The mirror was sinking in," "The weary world sinks deep into a hollow" — to take examples drawn from a central theme — no doubt refer, for the poet, to his constant sensation that he walked always on treacherous ground, that the earth under his feet was giving way.[5] In the mind of most readers these images will produce a nonspecific sensation of physical or emotional unease, which is experienced as valuable because its verbal expression is so complete. What words can truly encompass is, as Henri Michaux would say, "exorcised," not only for the poet but for the reader, each according to his need.

The recurring patterns of rhyme and rhythm in traditional verse function as a kind of incantation, making words seem inevitable and thus convincing at levels deeper than the rational. The form, however, is simply adopted for the occasion. Reverdy's poems have no external structure, but only the form secreted by the words, as certain organisms secrete their shells. Patternless rhyme and rhythm, like the spokes of a mobile, delineate the interplay of the words. Syntactic ambiguity, examples of which can be found everywhere in *Les Ardoises du toit*, forces the "subject" into the background:

>   The voices talking
> For so long was all that has come to pass
> The same . . .
> *A View from Long Ago*

>   And sip from transparent crystal
>   Air
>   And light
>   Gleams on the edge of the glass . . .
>   *Crossroad*

>   In my heart only vibrates space
>   *Beacon*

The poet is to be both concealed and revealed by his poem,[6] a structure that is its own multifaceted context.

Metaphor operates from the poet's mind to the reader's via the eye. Reverdy, throughout his life, insisted on the absolute priority of the eye over the ear, but the early poems are particularly dependent on being seen. The position of the words and the shape of the surrounding spaces amount, as he said, to a new kind of punctuation, indicating the relationship of parts to each other and to the whole, underlining a new kind of rhythm. The poem remains, however, exclusively a verbal structure; as an object for the eye it has no meaning, unless we should make an exception for the first page of *Les Ardoises du toit*, to which we will turn our attention.

As the page now appears, there is some suggestion of descent along an inclined plane in the first poem, and a contrasting horizontal stability in the second. This effect is more pronounced in the 1918 edition because the lines are more widely separated. The first poem was printed entirely in a very large dark type, elsewhere used for titles. The second poem is placed very far from the first, and printed in a much smaller and lighter type, again with a wider separation between the lines than we see now. The second poem is thus subordinate, further away, more fragile, and presents itself as an example: one individual slate on the ground. It is attached, nevertheless, by its subject, to the roof, the first poem, a verbal structure in the air. "The gutter is rimmed with diamonds" is a totally conventional, even exhausted metaphor that functions as a comparison. "The birds drink them" evokes a quality of diamonds incompatible with water-drops and, simultaneously, the natural world, never thirsty for metaphor. The result is not a comparison but an event, an event that can occur only in the mind and be expressed only in language that here, with an almost ostentatious simplicity (les oiseaux les boivent), summarizes its own powers and their limits. The reader may indeed experience a shock of pleasure, endlessly renewable because the poem makes contact with something at the core of human experience.

"Façade," which occupies the second page of the collection, may also be regarded as introductory. A façade is what one can see from the outside, that is, the reader's position, at least initially. Whatever physical form the word evokes, it will serve as a location for the poem's window, through which something also moves from outside in. The word *fenêtre*, if not, alas, *window*, has a complicated resonance containing *être* (to be) and possibly *naître* (to be born), both of them harmonious with Mallarmé's *fenêtre* which is access to and separation from *l'azur*, the absolute, or, in Reverdy's terminology, the light.

Many statements made by Reverdy would seem to reject double meanings based on sound. Yet, in citing Homer's "l'au-

rore aux doigts de rose" ("rosy-fingered dawn") as an example of
what poetry does in the world, he suggested that "rose" might be
considered also the flower, adding that an authentic image
should invite and accommodate all the associations of ideas it
arouses in the reader.[7] The example is particularly welcome
since it puts no restrictions on even a translated text. "Doigts de
rose" need only be seen on the page. But Reverdy, who wanted
his readers to be silent, could not have wished them unaware of
the sound of his words, especially those he so intricately rhymes.
"Façade" has four conspicuous rhymes in *-elle* which visually
may suggest a female person or a noun of feminine gender (*la
nouvelle*), and, for the ear, *aile* (wing) which would be appropriate
to the mysterious arrival "through the window" and the subse-
quent departure into the new day or the poem.

    La nouvelle itself may be something heard, the gentle voice;
in connection with *la Bonne Nouvelle*, an annunciation. It may
also be simply the light of the new day (*nouvelle journée*). The
direction indicated for the eyes would seem to be into the past,
toward gestures, *signes*, whether the act of writing or another
kind of attempted communication, but concealed behind a cur-
tain, an obstacle to light.

    Meanwhile, in both the past and the present of the poem,
the sun is rising. (The 1918 version has *le matin*, lower case,
placed closer to *un rideau* which emphasizes this simultaneity.)
But the morning's own façade, or face, seems to express disgust
and then a self-directed violence: the sun loses its outline in its
own radiance, and is blinded. The sun cannot see, but the poet
can. The last line of the poem, "Nous sommes deux sur le
chemin" ("There are two of us on the road"), is connected, by its
indentation, to no other. *Chemin* is related by rhyme to *main*
(hand) and *matin* (morning), a sequence suggesting that the road
may be the writing of the poem. The poet's companion is un-
identified. It has often been noted that Reverdy uses a variety of
personal pronouns to refer to aspects of himself. In this case,
however, *nous* may also refer to *la nouvelle* or to the reader, or to
both. *Signes* made in isolation are now coming into the light; the
road may lead through the day, but it certainly leads through the
poem which, as we have noted, will be a source of illumination
for an illuminating mind.

    This is not to say that everything will come out into the
light. Reverdy's poems quite often seem deliberately to go
beyond Wallace Stevens's statement that "Poetry must resist the
intelligence almost successfully." They include obscurities about

which only inconclusive speculation is possible. These may, however, be functional *as* obscurities. To whatever extent the reader participates, there remains, as in all communication, the mystery of the *other*. "Façade" offers a striking example, not readily made perceptible in English, in the *vous* of line four which is in immediate opposition to *tu* in the same sentence. The masculine participle, *pressé*, precludes its referring to *la nouvelle*. *Vous*, as used in formal address, may be intended to involve the reader, or, as a plural form, may indicate that the only one who *is* in a hurry is the poet, like Rimbaud, "pressé de trouver le lieu et la formule" ("in a hurry to find the place and the formula").

A reader who responds to a Reverdy poem will find that it gives an impression of coherence before he can explain how this is so. In "Patience," which is representative, there are two simultaneously presented sets of elements. From the one we are aware of emotions: a sense of isolation, tranquillity, hope, and discouragement; then separation again, in a more dramatic form: "The wall endlessly lengthens." The other relates to sound: those unidentified voices we encounter so often in this book, "tremble on the horizon" so that the verb, balanced between an auditory impression and a visual one, reduces them to what, in fact, they always were, a mere vibration. At the same time, "tremble," which could, after all, have been "vibrate," suggests fear.[8] Further on, these voices may be related to those of the people "inside," and to the effort to make words, meaning, and tone coincide. Here we also return to the theme of sound: vibration as opposed to the meaning which makes words heavier so that they "fall." (This may be why the slates will fall from the roof.) Eyelids move in response, perhaps, to this invisible and yet, since it has weight, physical phenomenon. Their motion is another form of vibration, coming between the eye and what it sees.

Vision is also a unifying theme: "one could see," "they are looking," "one does not see," the eyelids, the stranger watched and perhaps also watching. Verbs of motion provide another structural element: "were rising," "those who are going away," "pass," "fall," "rise," "move," "lengthen," and, at the very end of the poem, "stop." The tranquillity of the clearing is remembered in contrast to "nothing is clear inside my head." The stranger on the rutless road appears again on the black sidewalk where he, or it, comes to a stop. Perhaps it is he who has the patience of the title, perhaps it is the poet creating his subtly balanced structure, perhaps "patience" refers to the endless need to wait until hope can be more than a transient gleam of light. Or, rather, patience is involved in all of these.

The leitmotif of the journey occurs either directly or indirectly in nearly every poem of *Les Ardoises du toit*, beginning with the hazardous journey of the poem itself. The poet may be "on the road," as in "Façade" (but never sure it is the road he should have taken, as "Carrefour" so definitively states). He may also be immobile against a background of the physical world in movement, as in the fourth poem, "Réclame," where clouds are on the march toward "the other end of the world" (as precise a destination as we find), leaving a clear sky and "the moon to listen to you." A particularly interesting combination of motion and rest occurs in "On the Bank."

The opening words replace the expected *soleil couchant* (the setting sun) with "le soir couchant": "Evening, as it sets, closes a door." Other commentators see this analogy as directly successful, that is, actually bestowing on evening a discrete form, like the sun's. It seems more likely, however, to work indirectly; by presenting simultaneously to the reader's mind the two kinds of transition, sunset and the twilight turning to night, the amorphous quality of evening is emphasized. Similarly, in "Silence" the line "When the evening grows hard and falls" produces, in its return to the literal meaning of nightfall, a self-contradictory effect. The formlessness itself becomes more substantial. The oddity of the expression "soir couchant" may remind one also of an heraldic beast, another kind of shape the evening can and cannot assume.

It is darker when evening sets than when the sun sets. A closed door is a negation, an end of possibilities, presumably those of the preceding day. Someone is on the edge of the road, that is, no longer in transit, closed into the night, in the shadow, thus hidden. Also hidden is the life under the waters of the brook, but that unseen life, rather than simply being (*nous sommes*, we are), *se tient:* it is vigilant, emphatically self-contained, perhaps making itself as small as possible because it is threatened.

A brook is a kind of road, and its inhabitants, like the narrator and the reader, seem not to follow its course. There may be a remaining light, but we are not sure how to interpret what we see ("If that's one more line of light . . ."). And "line" makes the light also a kind of road, in the sky and on the page. The phrase *part à l'infini* means that the light is on its way to the infinite, where our minds cannot follow, and that it never stops departing, so that we have no need to follow. The second reading, difficult to reproduce in English, makes the line of light resemble the brook.

Both following the road and failing to do so may put one at risk. "The water rises like a kind of dust," "L'eau monte comme une poussière," a statement in many ways representative of Reverdy's subtle art. If he uses simile here, as he does so rarely, it is because the two elements are precisely not to combine. The simile, however, is merely the skeleton of the image. Dust is made to take the place of water through techniques whose effects will be mainly subliminal. The very gradual, almost silent rising of the water is suggested by the level rhythm of the words in combination with monotonous vowel sounds whose range is only between ō and ü. The dust, although sibilant, is not volatile; held down as if by the weight of the water, it creeps, but is none the less life-denying for that. "Comme *une* poussière" places it in a special, rather mysterious (the opposite of *commune*, common) category. If the water turns to dust, the life within it will be destroyed. Those "on the bank" will perhaps also be engulfed by something more frightening than water, and certainly by the silence which, larger than night, closes it as evening closes a door, or the poet his poem.

The theme of seeing, which Reverdy explores from many directions, often brings the spectator himself, rather than what he sees, into focus. "On the Bank" indicates the uncertainty of visual experience. In "Evening" "The knees of someone praying can't be seen" may be taken as a simple, if unexpected, observation, indicating primarily that someone was there to make it. One may read similarly, but with an ironic overtone, "From a distance the lips all seemed to be fervent and praying" ("Lightshade"). *Les Ardoises du toit* begins with a view from a distance toward the poems, the slates falling, the façade. The word *regard*, which we first encounter in "Point," the twenty-sixth poem, and which occurs frequently thereafter, may refer either to the expression in the eyes, as seen by someone else, or to the action of looking, directed toward the outside. In "Bêtes" we find both meanings: "His astonished eyes plumb the depths of the sky" . . . "I will always remember the look in your eyes." "Regard" is the title of the concluding poem, which subordinates to the idea of vision a number of other leitmotifs.

The poem begins in a visual perspective. Even before we

know who is "seated on the horizon," we know that there must be an observer for a horizon to exist. It is, in fact, "the others" who are going to sing, and who proceed to do so, if we may take the following past tense verb to indicate a passage of time during which "we" did not listen to the song, but rather "looked on" ("nous avons regardé"). The narrator's vision extended along the ruts in the dusty road, but "your look" ("ton regard") was a reproach. Although there are not a few poems in which *tu* seems clearly to designate another person, as in "Bêtes," here it seems to refer not to someone else but to another way of seeing. "Ton regard" would be, in this reading, the more authentic vision, that of the poet functioning as such, and, at the end of the poem, it totally displaces the other, that of "my eyes." The book itself has replaced its source in reality directly experienced. Thus the voice that goes on weeping has nevertheless become "better."

The poet's vision is left to deal with what it sees, experience that remains unreconstructed, at least for the moment, because this is the end of the last poem. We are told what it consists of: "tous ceux qui jamais t'offensèrent" (all those by whom the poet was ever humiliated, wounded or insulted). *Offensèrent* is linked by rhyme with *poussière* (dust) and *ornières* (ruts), suggesting that the narrator himself, with his excessively physical vision, is included among the offenders. The verb places the offense emphatically in the past (also, *derrière*). One assumes, with unwarranted optimism perhaps, that it will not be repeated, or only ineffectually. On the other hand, the poet now has his poems behind him, and in front of him this group, united by past hostility, which may or may not be giving him its attention. They are potential, although dubious, readers, or subjects, or both, and form, with the poet, another unity: *t'offensèrent*. The poet thus has, yet does not have, the final word.

Patricia Terry

Notes
  [1] Pierre Reverdy, *Cette Emotion appelée poésie*, Flammarion, 1974, p. 160.
  [2] Pierre Reverdy, *Nord-Sud*, Flammarion, 1975, p. 206.
  [3] *Cette Emotion appelée poésie*, p. 25.
  [4] *Nord-Sud*, p. 74.

[5] Robert Greene, "Pierre Reverdy," in *Six French Poets*, Princeton University Press, 1979, p. 62.

[6] Pierre Reverdy, *Note éternelle du présent*, Flammarion, 1973, p. 15.

[7] *Cette Emotion appelée poésie*, p. 46.

[8] Mary Ann Caws suggests that *voix* (voices) are also *voies* (roads), a reading that would add another coherent dimension. An example from "The Shadow of the Wall" might be mentioned in support of this reading: "Des bêtes qu'on ne voit pas/Voix" ("Invisible animals/Voices"). The two homonyms, although visually explicit, might argue for Reverdy's awareness of the third.

"Darkroom," typeset by Pierre Reverdy for the 1918 edition of *Les Ardoises du toit*. The poet's revisions are written in by hand. (Courtesy of the Bibliothèque Littéraire Jacques Doucet).

Poems

Sur chaque ardoise
             qui glissait du toit
                on
           avait écrit
                un poème

La gouttière est bordée de diamants
             les oiseaux les boivent

On every slate
        sliding from the roof
           someone
          had written
              a poem

The gutter is rimmed with diamonds
                the birds drink them

FAÇADE

Par la fenêtre
            La nouvelle
Entre
            Vous n'êtes pas pressé
Et la voix douce qui t'appelle
Indique où il faut regarder
            Rappelle-toi
                        Le jour se lève
      Les signes que faisait ta main
Derrière un rideau
                        Le matin
A fait une grimace brève
Le soleil crève sa prunelle
      Nous sommes deux sur le chemin

FACADE

Through the window
                    Something new
Comes in
            There is plenty of time
And the gentle voice calling you
Lets you know where to look
                    Remember
                            It's getting light
            The gestures of your hand
Behind a curtain
                            Morning
Suddenly made a face
The sun bursts the apple of its eye
            There are two of us on the road

RÉCLAME

Hangar monté
                la porte ouverte
Le ciel
        En haut deux mains se sont offertes
Les yeux levés
                Une voix monte
Les toits se sont mis à trembler
Le vent lance des feuilles mortes
Et les nuages retardés
Marchent vers l'autre bout du monde
Qui se serait mis à siffler
Dans le calme d'un soir d'été
Le chant
        L'oiseau
                Les étoiles
Et la lune pour t'écouter

HAWKING

Raised hangar
                    the door open
The sky
            Up there two hands extended
Lifted eyes
            A voice rises
The roofs have begun to tremble
The wind launches dead leaves
And the clouds delayed
Set out for the other end of the world
Which perhaps had begun to whistle
In the calm of a summer evening
The song
            The bird
                        The stars
And the moon to listen to you

See note on p. 169.

MATIN

La fontaine coule sur la place du port d'été
Le soleil déridé brille au travers de l'eau
Les voix qui murmuraient sont bien plus lointaines
Il en reste encore quelques frais lambeaux
J'écoute le bruit
                  Mais elles où sont-elles
Que sont devenus leurs paniers fleuris
Les murs limitaient la profondeur de la foule
Et le vent dispersa les têtes qui parlaient
Les voix sont restées à peu près pareilles
Les mots sont posés à mes deux oreilles
Et le moindre cri les fait s'envoler

MORNING

The fountain flows in the square of the summer harbor
Smooth-browed the sun is gleaming through the water
Those murmuring voices are very much farther away
Just a few cool fragments remain
For me to hear
                        But they where are they
What has become of their baskets full of flowers
The walls determined the thickness of the crowd
And the wind dispersed the heads in conversation
The voices are really very much the same
The words have come to rest on my two ears
And the slightest outcry makes them fly away

FEU

Enfin le vent plus libre passe
La pointe fléchit sur sa trace
Une vague s'efface plus loin
Sur le champ le plan monte
                    Le ciel s'incline lentement
Un lambeau de nuage flotte
Plus sombre par-dessus le mur
                    L'espace s'agrandit
Et là devant
              Quelqu'un qui n'a rien dit
              Deux yeux
              Une double lumière
        Qui vient de franchir la barrière
              En s'abattant

FIRE

At last the freer wind passes
The tip bends down in its path
A more distant wave surrenders
Thereupon the field's level rises
                    The sky bows slowly down
A fragment of cloud floats
Darker above the wall
                    Space expands
And there in front
                    Someone who hasn't said anything
                    Two eyes
                    A double light
        Just forced its way through the barrier
                    By knocking itself out

See note

GRAND-ROUTE

Le feu est presque éteint
   Et devant quelqu'un pleure
Où passe cette main
   Dont la chaleur demeure

Il fait nuit
   Les vitres se fondent

Si la maison disparaissait
   Avec nous derrière les arbres
Quelqu'un encore resterait
Une voix douce chanterait
      Et l'ombre du temps s'en irait
Le soir
   Faire le tour du monde

HIGHWAY

The fire has almost gone out
       And close to it someone in tears
Where has that hand moved on
      Whose warmth is still here

It is dark
      The windows melt

If the house were to disappear
      With us behind the trees
Someone would still remain
A gentle voice would be singing
           And the shadow of time would go away
In the evening
      To travel the world

LE SOIR

Jour à jour ta vie est un immeuble qui s'élève
Des fenêtres fermées des fenêtres ouvertes
    Et la porte noire au milieu
Ce qui brille dans ta figure
                   Les yeux
      Tristes les souvenirs glissent sur
      ta poitrine
Devant part vers en haut l'espoir
La douceur du repos qui revient chaque soir
Tu es assis devant la porte
    Tête inclinée
             Dans l'ombre qui s'étend
Le calme qui descend
Une prière monte
On ne voit pas les genoux de celui qui prie

IN THE EVENING

Day by day your life is a building going up
There are closed windows open windows
    and the black door in between
What illuminates your face
                    Your eyes
    Sad the memories gliding over
    your breast
In front there is hope ascending
The sweetness of rest returning in the evening
You sit in front of the door
    With your head bowed
                  In the widening shadow
The calm drifting down
A prayer rises
The knees of someone praying can't be seen

AUBERGE

Un œil se ferme

    Au fond plaquée contre le mur
    la pensée qui ne sort pas

    Des idées s'en vont pas à pas

   On pourrait mourir
Ce que je tiens entre mes bras pourrait partir

   Un rêve

  L'aube à peine née qui s'achève
  Un cliquetis
Les volets en s'ouvrant l'ont abolie

    Si rien n'allait venir

Il y a un champ où l'on pourrait encore courir
               Des étoiles à n'en plus finir
    Et ton ombre au bout de l'avenue
        Elle s'efface

On n'a rien vu
De tout ce qui passait on n'a rien retenu
Autant de paroles qui montent
Des contes qu'on n'a jamais lus
               Rien
Les jours qui se pressent à la sortie
    Enfin la cavalcade s'est évanouie

En bas entre les tables où l'on jouait aux cartes

INN

An eye closes

> Deep inside and flat against the wall
> the thought which doesn't go out

> Ideas step by step go their way

Death could happen
What I hold in my arms could slip away

A dream

Dawn at its birth dies out
In a clatter
Of opening shutters annulled

> If nothing were going to come

There's a field where we could still run
Unlimited stars
And your shadow where the avenue comes to an end
Vanishing
We have seen nothing
Of all that was passing we held on to nothing
So many words rising
Stories we never read
Nothing
The days in a rush for the exit
At last the cavalcade has faded out

Down there between the tables where we played cards

See note

CADRAN

Sur la lune
          s'inscrit
              Un mot
La lettre la plus grande en haut
Elle est humide comme un œil
La moitié se ferme
         Et le ciel
              Se couvre
      Un lourd rideau qu'on ouvre
Sans bruit
          Une lumière luit
Rapide
C'est une autre lueur à présent
      qui me guide

DIAL

On the moon
            is inscribed
                      A word
With its tallest letter on top
Moist as an eye
Half of it closes
           And the sky
                        Clouds over
   A heavy curtain is opened
Soundlessly
                A quick light
Gleams
It's another glow just now
    that guides me

ABAT-JOUR

Autour de la table
                  Au bord de l'ombre
Aucun d'eux ne remue beaucoup
Et quelqu'un parle tout à coup
Il fait froid dehors
          Mais là c'est le calme
Et la lumière les unit
                  Le feu pétille
Une étincelle
          Les mains se sont posées
          Plus bleues sur le tapis
Derrière le rayon une tête qui lit
          Un souffle qui s'échappe à peine
Tout s'endort
Le silence traîne
          Mais il faut encore rester
La vitre reproduit le tableau
          La famille
De loin toutes les lèvres ont l'air d'être ferventes et
    de prier

LIGHTSHADE

Around the table
          On the shadow's edge
Each one of them quite motionless
And someone abruptly speaks
It's cold outside
  But here it's peaceful
And the light holds them together
          The fire crackles
A spark
        The hands have come to rest
        Bluer on top of the tablecloth
Behind the beam of light a head reads
        Nearly holding its breath
Everything's falling asleep
The silence drags on
        But still it is not time to go
The windowpane mirrors the scene
        The family
From a distance the lips all seem to be fervent and
  praying

See note

TARD DANS LA NUIT . . .

La couleur que décompose la nuit
La table où ils se sont assis
Le verre en cheminée
        La lampe est un cœur qui se vide
C'est une autre année
     Une nouvelle ride
Y aviez-vous déjà pensé
        La fenêtre déverse un carré bleu
La porte est plus intime
     Une séparation
        Le remords et le crime
Adieu je tombe
Dans l'angle doux des bras qui me reçoivent
Du coin de l'œil je vois tous ceux qui boivent
     Je n'ose pas bouger
Ils sont assis
        La table est ronde
Et ma mémoire aussi
Je me souviens de tout le monde
Même de ceux qui sont partis

LATE AT NIGHT . . .

The color night disintegrates
They are sitting around the table
The chimney glass
          The lamp giving out like a heart
It's another year
   One more wrinkle
Had you thought of that before
          The window pours out a square of blue
More personal is the door
   A separation
          Remorse and crime
Farewell I'm falling
Into the gentle angle of open arms
I see the drinkers from the corner of my eye
          To move could be dangerous
They sit there
               The table is round
My memory is too
I remember everyone
Even those who have gone

SUR LE TALUS

Le soir couchant ferme une porte
Nous sommes au bord du chemin
Dans l'ombre
      près du ruisseau où tout se tient

Si c'est encore une lumière
        La ligne part à l'infini

L'eau monte comme une poussière

     Le silence ferme la nuit

ROUTE

Sur le seuil personne
        Ou ton ombre
Un souvenir qui resterait
La route passe
    Et les arbres parlent plus près
Qu'y a-t-il derrière
        Un mur
            des voix
Les nuages qui s'élevèrent
Au moment où je passais là
Et tout le long une barrière
        Où sont ceux qui n'entreront pas

ON THE BANK

Evening as it sets closes a door
We are on the edge of the road
In the shadow
   close to the brook where everything waits

If that's one more line of light
       It's heading for infinity

The water rises like a kind of dust

      Silence closes the night

ROAD

On the threshold no one
         Or your shadow
A lingering memory
The road passes by
    And the trees come closer as they talk
What is there behind
       A wall
            voices
The clouds that lifted
Just as I was passing by
And all along a barrier
        Where are those who shall not enter

SUR LE SEUIL

Dans le coin où elle s'est blottie
                Tristesse ou vide
Le vent tourne
             On entend un cri
Personne n'a voulu se plaindre
Mais la lampe vient de s'éteindre
         Et passe sans faire de bruit
Une main tiède
        Sur tes paupières
        Où pèse la journée finie
Tout se dresse
        Et dans le monde qui se presse
Les objets mêlés à la nuit
           La forme que j'avais choisie
Si la lumière
        Revivait conme on se réveille
Il resterait dans mon oreille
La voix joyeuse qui la veille
En rentrant m'avait poursuivi

ON THE THRESHOLD

Where she is huddled into a corner
                   Emptiness or pain
The wind circles
                 A cry is heard
No one went to complain
But the lamp has just gone out
              And silently passes
A hand warm
          On your eyelids
             Weighed down by the end of the day
Everything stiffens upright
            And in the rush of the crowd
Where objects merge into night
              The form that I had in mind
If light
         Came to life again as we do out of sleep
There would remain in my ear
The joyful voice that the day before
Tried to follow me all the way home

ABÎME

Je m'attendais à tout ce qui peut arriver
La tête en bas
          Les pieds touchant la tête
Et tout ce qui dans l'angle remuait
Contre le mur
          En face et par côté
La glace qui s'éteint s'était mise à trembler
Il y avait une lumière
                    Autrefois
Et la figure que je vois
                    Minuit
          Serait-ce l'heure
Sous le toit la gouttière pleure
Et le train au loin qui criait
La chambre s'étendait bien plus loin que les murs

Alors on aurait pu m'atteindre
          Ou même j'aurais pu tomber

Le monde pour dormir se renversait

ABYSS

I was expecting anything that can happen
Upside down
      Feet touching my head
And whatever stirred in the corner
Against the wall
      Opposite and to one side
As it went out the mirror began to tremble
There was a light
         Once
And the face I can see
        Midnight
    Would this be the time
Under the roof the rainspout weeps
And the train crying out in the distance
The bedroom extended far beyond the walls

They could have gotten to me then
    I could even have fallen

The world ready for sleep was turning over

See note

DÉPART

L'horizon s'incline
        Les jours sont plus longs
        Voyage
    Un cœur saute dans une cage
        Un oiseau chante
        Il va mourir
Une autre porte va s'ouvrir
        Au fond du couloir
        Où s'allume
        Une étoile
Une femme brune
        La lanterne du train qui part

DEPARTURE

The horizon leans down
            The days are longer
            Travelling
    A heart leaps up in its cage
            A bird sings
            It is going to die
There will be another door open
        At the end of the corridor
            Now glows
            A star
A woman with dark hair
        The lantern of the departing train

UNE ÉCLAIRCIE

Il fait plus noir
          Les yeux se ferment
La prairie se dressait plus claire
  Dans l'air il y avait un mouchoir
Et tu faisais des signes
          Ta main sortait sous la manche du soir
Je voulais franchir la barrière
       Quelque chose me retenait
Le cri venait de loin
      Par-derrière la nuit
Et tout ce qui s'avance
         Et tout ce que je fuis
Encore
    Je me rappelle
La rue que le matin inondait de soleil

A BREAK IN THE CLOUDS

It's getting darker
          Eyes close
The plain was rising up brighter
     There was a handkerchief in the air
And you were beckoning
          Your hand emerging from an evening sleeve
I wanted to cross the barrier
         Something was holding me back
The cry was coming from far away
        From the other side of the night
And all that comes forward
         And all that I flee
Still
        I remember
The street that morning filled to the brim with sunlight

See note

LENDEMAIN

Une ombre était passée ce soir sur le fronton
Sur la bande du ciel
        Et sur la plaine ouverte
        Où tombait un rayon
Elle restait immobile
        Aurait-on pu de loin
    Entendre seulement le cri d'une sirène
Et tout ce qui marchait
Sur la terre et dans l'air
Plus vite
        Elle s'envolait
        Il ne restait plus bas
        Que les gens inhabiles
        Ceux qui les retenaient
Et moi
        Regardant la lumière tremblante
La rue qui se laissait aller
Tout seul devant ma vie passée
Et par où commencer le jour qui se présente

NEXT DAY

This evening a shadow passed over the pediment
Over the strip of sky
        And the open plain
        Where a ray of light was falling
To stand immobile
        Could one only have heard
   In the distance a siren's cry
And all that was moving
On the earth and in the air
More quickly
        It flew away
        Nothing was left lower down
        But the incapable people
        Those who were holding them back
And myself
        To watch the light tremble
The street let itself go
All alone to face the life that I've lived
And where to begin with the day that is coming to meet me

RONDE NOCTURNE

             Le timbre vient de loin
Les mondes se rapprochent
Sur les bords du clocher des étoiles s'accrochent
             Dans le coin des cheminées fument
Ce sont des bougies qui s'allument
Quelqu'un monte
             Les cloches vont sonner
Un nuage en passant les a fait remuer
A présent on a l'habitude
             Personne n'est plus étonné
Les yeux mesurent l'altitude
             Où vous êtes placé
Un cœur libre s'est envolé
             On peut encore choisir la place
             Où l'on pourrait se reposer
             Après avoir longtemps marché
Plus bas il reste une surface
             Dans la nuit
On écoutait
             Serait-ce lui
A l'horizon sans bruit quelqu'un montait au ciel
L'escalier craque
             Il est artificiel
C'est une parabole ou une passerelle
L'heure qui s'échappait ne bat plus que d'une aile

NOCTURNAL ROUND

The resonance comes from afar
The worlds draw closer together
On the bell tower's edges cling stars
Chimneys smoke in the corner
They are candles coming alight
Someone is climbing up
The bells are about to ring
Stirred by a passing cloud
We are used to it now
No one is astonished any more
Eyes measure the altitude
Of your station
A free heart has flown away
We can still choose our own places
Where it would be possible to rest
After walking a long time
Lower down there is one more surface
In the night
We were listening
Perhaps it is he
Soundless on the horizon someone was climbing to the sky
The stairway cracks
It is an artificial thing
A gangplank or a parabola
Now the escaping hour beats only one wing

SON DE CLOCHE

                Tout s'est éteint
Le vent passe en chantant
                Et les arbres frissonnent
Les animaux sont morts
Il n'y a plus personne
                            Regarde
Les étoiles ont cessé de briller
                La terre ne tourne plus
Une tête s'est inclinée
                Les cheveux balayant la nuit
Le dernier clocher resté debout
                Sonne minuit

SORTIE

Le Vestiaire
                Le Portemanteau
                            La lumière
Au mur des têtes inclinées
                Un rayon d'électricité
La voix qui chante
                Un cœur qui s'est ouvert
Dans la salle éclatante
                Un soir d'hiver
La foule que le feu déverse
Sur le trottoir et sous l'averse
Les diamants renvoyant les éclats
Dans la nuit le silence plane

Et c'est une voiture qui l'emporte

SOUND OF A BELL

All the lights are out
The wind passes singing
                    And the trees shiver
The animals are dead
There is no one left
                    Look
The stars are not shining now
                    Or the earth turning
A head has bowed
                    Hair sweeps the night
The last bell tower upright
                    Strikes midnight

EXIT

The Cloakroom
                    The Coatrack
                              The light
Bowed heads on the wall
                    A beam of electricity
The voice singing
                    A heart opened up
In the dazzling room
                    One winter evening
The crowd that the fire pours out
On the sidewalk and under the sudden rain
The diamonds' flashing reply
Silence glides on the night

And a carriage takes all

AIR

Oubli
porte fermée
Sur la terre inclinée
Un arbre tremble
Et seul
Un oiseau chante

Sur le toit
Il n'y a plus de lumière
Que le soleil

Et les signes que font tes doigts

POSTE

Pas une tête ne dépasse

Un doigt se lève
Puis c'est la voix que l'on connaît
Un signal
une note brève
Un homme part
Là-haut un nuage qui passe
Personne ne rentre
Et la nuit garde son secret

AIR

Something forgotten
closed door
On the sloping earth
A tree trembles
All alone
A bird is singing

On the roof
All the light left
Is the sun

And the gestures your fingers make

POST

Not one head sticks over
A finger is raised
Then comes the voice we know
A signal
a short note
A man goes away
Up there a passing cloud
No one comes home
And the night keeps its secret

ORAGE

La fenêtre
           Un trou vivant où l'éclair bat
Plein d'impatience
              Le bruit a percé le silence
On ne sait plus si c'est la nuit
           La maison tremble
Quel mystère
La voix qui chante va se taire
Nous étions plus près
                    Au-dessous
Celui qui cherche
           Plus grand que ce qu'il cherche
Et c'est tout
              Soi
Sous le ciel ouvert
              Fendu
Un éclat où le souffle est resté
                    Suspendu

STORM

The window
          A living hole where the lightning beats
Full of impatience
          The noise has pierced the silence
We no longer know if it's night
          The house trembles
So mysteriously
The voice that is singing will cease
We were closer
          Underneath
The seeker
          Greater than what he seeks
And that's all
          Oneself
Under the open sky
          Split in two
A brilliance whose flight was left hanging
          In the air

MIRACLE

Tête penchée
                 Cils recourbés
Bouche muette
Les lampes se sont allumées
Il n'y a plus qu'un nom
                     Que l'on a oublié
La porte se serait ouverte
Et je n'oserais pas entrer
                   Tout ce qui se passe derrière

On parle
           Et je peux écouter

Mon sort était en jeu dans la pièce à côté

MIRACLE

Bowed head
                    Upturned eyelashes
Mute mouth
Light now from the lamps
The only thing left is a name
                    They have forgotten
Were the door to open
I would not dare go in
                    All that is happening behind

They are talking
          And I can listen

My future was at stake in the next room

POINTE

Au coin du bois
Quelqu'un se cache
On pourrait approcher sans bruit
Vers le vide ou vers l'ennemi
En tombant la nuit s'est fendue
Deux bras sont restés étendus
Dans l'ombre un regard fixe
                    Un éclair éperdu
          Pour aller plus loin vers la croix
Tout ce qu'on voit
          Tout ce qu'on croit
C'est ce qui part
Là ou ailleurs sans qu'on le sache
Avec la peur d'aller trop près
Du ravin noir où tout s'efface

OUTPOST

On the edge of the woods
Someone is hiding
We could making no sound approach
Nearer the abyss or the enemy
As it fell night split apart
Two arms remain extended
In the shadow a fixed stare
                    A flash of frenzied light
        To go on toward the cross
Everything one sees
            Everything one believes
That's what leaves
There or elsewhere and not to our knowledge
With the fear of going too close
To the black ravine where everything is wiped out

SECRET

La cloche vide
Les oiseaux morts
Dans la maison où tout s'endort
Neuf heures

La terre se tient immobile
On dirait que quelqu'un soupire
Les arbres ont l'air de sourire
L'eau tremble au bout de chaque feuille
Un nuage traverse la nuit

Devant la porte un homme chante

La fenêtre s'ouvre sans bruit

MINUTE

Il n'est pas encore revenu

Mais qui dans la nuit est entré

La pendule les bras en croix
S'est arrêtée

SECRET

The bell is empty
The birds dead
In the house where everything is falling asleep
Nine o'clock

The earth stands immobile
That sounds like a sigh
The trees look as if they are smiling
Water trembles at the tip of every leaf
A cloud moves across the night

In front of the door a man is singing

The window opens not making a sound

MINUTE

He hasn't come back yet
Who has entered the depths of the night
The clock with its arms wide open
Stopped

See note

BÊTES

Tu regardes en passant l'animal enchaîné
                    Il part de son élan
L'exil entre les haies
          Son œil sonde le ciel d'un regard étonné
                    La tête contre la barrière
Vers ce reflet de l'infini
                    L'immensité
Prisonnier autant que toi-même
L'ennui ne te quittera pas
Mais je me souviendrai toujours de
                         ton regard
          Et de ta voix
                    terriblement humaine

ANIMALS

You give a passing glance to the beast in chains
                         His leap is beyond his power
Exile between hedges
      His astonished eyes plumb the sky
                    His head against the bars
Toward that hint of the infinite
                         Immensity
A prisoner just as you are
Boredom will never leave you
But I will always remember
                  the look in your eyes
       And your voice
          so terribly human

RIVES

La pièce est courte et l'acte est long
As-tu regardé par-derrière
                    Le miroir s'enfonçait
On y voyait une ombre
De tous ceux qui sont morts on ne sait plus le nombre
Il y avait un enfant pleurant près d'un ruisseau
Et le vent riant dans les branches
Les feuilles s'envolaient
                    Une larme tomba
Quel cri en passant sur la rive
                    Faisait frissonner l'eau
Un oiseau
En dessous
            un trou
                    l'œil fonce sans limite
Et que trouvera-t-on au bout
Un paysage fermé
            Une femme endormie
            La toile d'araignée
                    Un hamac transparent
Balance un point de plus dans le ciel étoilé

SHORES

The play is short and the act is long
Have you looked at it from behind
                      The mirror was sinking in
With a visible shadow
So many are dead their number who can know
There was a child weeping near a stream
And the wind laughing in branches
Whose leaves were flying away
                      A tear fell down
What cry passing over the shore
                Made the water shiver
A bird
Underneath
        a hole
                the eye is free to plunge into
And what will be found at the end
A private landscape
                  A woman asleep
                  The spiderweb
                        A transparent hammock
Swaying one more point in the starry sky

NOMADE

La porte qui ne s'ouvre pas
La main qui passe
Au loin un verre qui se casse
La lampe fume
Les étincelles qui s'allument
Le ciel est plus noir
Sur les toits

Quelques animaux
Sans leur ombre

Un regard
Une tache sombre

La maison où l'on n'entre pas

NOMAD

The door that will not open
The passing hand
         A glass that breaks in the distance
      Smoke from the lamp
And sparks lighting up
         The sky grows dark
            Along the roof tops

Animals here and there
Shadowless
                  A look
            A dark spot

The house we do not enter

LA JETÉE

Les étoiles sont derrière le mur
Dedans saute un cœur qui voudrait sortir
Aime le moment qui passe
          A force ta mémoire est lasse
D'écouter des cadavres de bruits
Dans le silence
          Rien ne vit
Au fond de l'eau l'image s'emprisonne
Au bord du ciel une cloche qui sonne
La voile est un morceau du port qui se détache

Tu restes là
          Tu regardes ce qui s'en va
Quelqu'un chante et tu ne comprends pas
La voix vient de plus haut
                    L'homme vient de plus loin
          Tu voudrais respirer à peine
Et l'autre aspirerait le ciel tout d'une haleine

JETTY

The stars are behind the wall
Inside leaps a heart that would like to go out
Loves the moment passing
            Weary no doubt your memory
Of hearing cadavers of sound
In the silence
            Nothing's alive
The image finds an underwater cell
On the border of the sky resounds a bell
The sail is a piece of the harbor moving away

There you stay
            You watch what is leaving
Someone sings and you don't understand
The voice comes from higher up
                The man from a more distant place
            You aspire to breathe less and less
And the other would draw in the whole sky on one breath

SILENCE

On parlait encore là derrière
Des hommes passaient deux à deux
C'était peut-être une prière
Qui montait des cœurs du milieu
Entre les murs de la clairière
Une voix qui tinte sur l'eau
L'oiseau prend un autre chemin
Et réveillée par le matin
      La tête sombre
Personne ne connaît le nombre
De ceux qui passent
Entre le mur et le jardin
     Quand le soir devient dur et tombe
        Au loin
On entend le sifflet d'un train

SILENCE

They were still talking there behind
Men were passing in pairs
Perhaps it was a prayer
That rose from the hearts in between
The walls around the clearing
A voice that chimes on the water
The bird goes another way
And awakened by the morning
                    The leaden head
No one can say
How many pass
Between the garden and the wall
                    When evening grows hard and falls
                         Far away
We hear the whistle of a train

See note

L'OMBRE DU MUR

Un œil crevé par une plume
Larme qui tombe de la lune
                Un lac
Le monde rentre dans un sac
                La nuit
Les cyprès font le même signe
En blanc la route les souligne
Le paysage hivernal est bleu
                        Les doigts tremblent
Deux grands carrés qui se ressemblent
Les ombres dansent au milieu
Des bêtes qu'on ne voit pas
                Des voix

Tout le long du chemin
                        Il pleut

THE SHADOW OF THE WALL

An eye with a quill through its back
A tear that comes from the moon
      A lake
The world finds its home in a sack
      After dark
The cypress trees all give one sign
That the highway's white blank underlines
The hibernal landscape is blue
      Fingers tremble
A big square another resembles
Shadows dance between the two
Invisible animals
      Voices

The length of the road
               Rain falls

VEILLÉE

Entre la maison et le ciel
                    Tout se gonfle
Car le vent souffle
Les étoiles montent de la cheminée
Une à une elles se sont fixées
Sur le fond
                    Une belle troupe
                              danse
Mais quelques-uns voudraient descendre
On repassera pour vous prendre
                              Ce soir
Le jour s'était levé plus tard
Une fatigue bien plus grande
Il faudrait rester plus longtemps
                    Nuage qui suit le courant
De la lumière qui s'écaille
Horizon déformé bouche qui bâille

EVENING VIGIL

Between the house and the heavens
                                All balloons
As the wind blows
The stars rise up from the chimney
One by one they stand determined
On the backdrop
                    A handsome troup
                                    dances
But there are those who would like to get down
We will call for you next time around
                                This evening
The sun had arisen later
A much greater fatigue
We would have to stay longer
                    Cloud that follows the tide
Of the scaling light
Distorted horizon mouth yawning wide

See note

SOLEIL

    Quelqu'un vient de partir
Dans la chambre
        Il reste un soupir
La vie déserte

     La rue
       Et la fenêtre ouverte
Un rayon de soleil
Sur la pelouse verte

EN FACE

     Au bord du toit
       Un nuage danse
Trois gouttes d'eau pendent à
              la gouttière
Trois étoiles
         Des diamants
Et vos yeux brillants qui regardent
    Le soleil derrière la vitre

    Midi

SUN

    Someone has just left
In the room
        Remains a sigh
Life deserted

    The street
       And the open window
One ray of sunlight
On the green lawn

ACROSS THE WAY

    On the edge of the roof
       A cloud is dancing
Three waterdrops hang from
             the gutter
Three stars
        Diamonds
And your eyes' brilliance watching
   The sun behind the windowpane

    Noon

SENTINELLE

La cheminée garde le toit
Comme le sommet la montagne
Le ciel passe derrière et le nuage bas
Contre l'œil qui regarde
       Minuit
Il reste au fond de l'air encore un peu de bruit
Une sourde chanson qui monte
Ce qu'on entend est plus joli
Les yeux se ferment
             On pourrait mourir

       Le reste n'a pas pu sortir
A cause de la peur on referme la porte
    Cette émotion était trop forte
La lueur qui baisse et remonte
         On dirait un sein qui bat

SENTINEL

The chimney keeps watch on the roof
As the summit the mountain
The sky passes behind and the low cloud
Level with the watching eye
          Midnight
There is still a little noise in the depths of the air
A muffled song rising
What we hear is more attractive
Eyes close
              Death could happen

          The rest didn't get out
Because of fear the door has been closed again
    That was too strong an emotion
The glow that rises and falls
              Like the pulse of a breast

CIEL ÉTOILÉ

Un arbre orienté vers le ciel
            Cette procession sombre
On éclaire le monde avec des bougies
Tout se tient trop loin et dans l'ombre
Un bruit de pas trouble la nuit

            Le mur se détache lentement
Et son ombre fait une tache
Contre la terre qui descend
Vers la rivière où l'on entend
      Le rire de cristal des roches

Un rayon blanc s'accroche en haut
      La nuit se balance un moment
Quelque chose tombe dans l'eau
            Une pluie d'étoiles

STARRY SKY

A tree oriented toward the sky
That somber procession
Candles are all the world's light
Everything keeps its distance and in the shadows
The noise of a footstep disturbs the night

The wall disconnects itself slowly
And its shadow makes a spot
Where the earth is coming down
Toward the river and its sound
The crystalline laughter of rocks

A white light ray hangs from on high
The night for a moment sways
Something falls into the water
A rain of stars

JOUEURS

Sa main tendue est une coquille où il pleut
Et l'eau sous la gouttière
                    fait un bruit de métal
Derrière le rideau une figure rouge
Dans l'air blanc matinal
          La fenêtre s'ouvre pour parler
Dans la cour le violon grince comme une clef
Et en face de l'homme le mur tient son sérieux
Il pleut sur la tête du joueur
          Il est vieux
Le chien malveillant le regarde
              Et puis c'est un enfant qui court
                      Sans prendre garde
                          Où il va

PLAYERS

It is raining in the shell of his outstretched hand
And the water below the gutter
                              makes a metallic sound
Behind the curtain a ruddy face
In the white early morning air
        The window opens to speak
The violin grates in the courtyard like a key
And the wall across from the man refrains from laughing
It is raining on the player's head
        He is old
The ill-tempered dog keeps its eye on him
        And then there's a child running by
                        Heedless
                            Of where he is going

LE MÊME NUMÉRO

Les yeux à peine ouverts
        La main sur l'autre rive
Le ciel
      Et tout ce qui arrive
La porte s'inclinait
        Une tête dépasse
Dans le cadre
Et par les volets
On peut regarder à travers
Le soleil prend toute la place
Mais les arbres sont toujours verts
         Une heure tombe
         Il fait plus chaud
Et les maisons sont plus petites
Ceux qui passaient allaient moins vite
Et regardaient toujours en haut
        La lampe à présent nous éclaire
En regardant plus loin
Et nous pouvions voir la lumière
         Qui venait
Nous étions contents
        Le soir

Devant l'autre demeure où quelqu'un nous attend

THAT NUMBER AGAIN

Eyes scarcely open
                One hand on the other shore
The sky
          And all that happens
The door was leaning down
            A head sticks over
Inside the frame
And the shutters
One can see through
The sun takes up all the room
But the trees are green just the same
                  An hour falls
                  It's getting warmer
And the houses smaller
The passersby were slowing down
They kept looking upward
              Now we're illuminated by the lamp
Looking further
We could see the light
          Coming
We were happy
          In the evening

In front of the other dwelling where someone awaits us

See note

AILE

Un souffle sec vient de plus loin
Les ailes noires se balancent
Rien ne part
Au chemin tournant
Les ardeurs du jour se délassent
La maison lourde dort
Les lumières s'éteignent
Dans le jardin deux arbres mourants
Qui s'étreignent
Il parle
Et l'autre pleure
Le soir
Il est onze heures
Et l'oiseau sans forme est parti
L'Ame aux ailes trop courtes
On a détruit le nid
Dans l'air froid quelque chose passe
Un léger bruit monte plus haut
Un rêve prudent qui se cache

WING

A dry breath from further on
The black wings trim their flight
Nothing leaves
On the winding road
The heat of the day relaxes
The heavy house sleeps on
The lights go out
In the garden two dying trees
Embrace
One talks
And the other weeps
In the evening
It's eleven o'clock
And the formless bird has left
The Soul whose wings are too short
They've destroyed the nest
Something passes through the cold air
A slight noise rises higher
A prudent dream going to hide

See note

RUE

Il faudrait passer là devant
       Paroles que le vent emporte
Combien nous faudra-t-il de temps
Encore une minute et je suis là
       Je reste seul contre la porte
Les arbres auront frissonné
       Si un nuage lourd s'arrête
Devant la porte refermée
Et sous le ciel
       Les heures passent
Moi j'oublierai même mon nom
       Sur le trottoir où ils sont nés
Les oiseaux crient
       D'autres voix roulent
La cloche s'est mise à sonner
       Et toutes les têtes qui tournent
En s'en allant m'auront parlé

STREET

We would have to pass in front
                Words carried off by the wind
How much will be enough time
One minute more and there I am
                        Alone with my back to the door
The trees must have shivered
                If a heavy cloud comes to a stop
In front of the door closed again
And under the sky
                The hours pass by
I'll even forget my own name
                On the sidewalk where they were born
The birds are crying
                Other voices roll on
The bell has begun to ring
                And all the heads that turn
As they leave will have spoken to me

CARREFOUR

S'arrêter devant le soleil
                              Après la chute ou le réveil
        Quitter la cuirasse du temps
Se reposer sur un nuage blanc
Et boire au cristal transparent
                    De l'air
                              De la lumière
Un rayon sur le bord du verre
Ma main déçue n'attrape rien
Enfin tout seul j'aurai vécu
Jusqu'au dernier matin

Sans qu'un mot m'indiquât quel fut le bon chemin

CROSSROAD

To stop in front of the sun
                              After the fall or the waking up
    Once the armor of time is shed
To take a white cloud for a bed
And sip from transparent crystal
                    Air
                    And light
Gleams on the edge of the glass where
Nothing fills my disappointed hand
So I'll have lived all alone
Up to the final day

Not a word to let me know which one was the right way

PHARE

Plus loin le verre blanc cassa
Les yeux au plafond se levèrent
Sur le ciel d'aujourd'hui
Un soleil faux qui luit
Un rayon dans la glace
Où mon portrait grimace
A l'envers
Et du grand livre ouvert
L'oiseau qui s'envola
Sortait d'une cage sans porte
De toute la production morte
Du premier jour qui se leva
Au nôtre il n'y a pas de place
Dans mon cœur seul vibre l'espace
Et c'est tout ce qui ne va pas

BEACON

The clear glass broke further on
Eyes rose toward the ceiling
On the sky today
A fake sun gleams
Bright ray in the mirror
Where my portrait makes a face
Wrong way around
And from the great open book
The bird flew away
Out of a doorless cage
For all that has come and gone
Ever since the initial dawn
Up to now there is no place
In my heart only vibrates space
Nothing else is wrong

EXOTISME

Un profil immortel sur le fronton
A Bornéo ou au delà
            Les rivières sont gelées
Les animaux courent sur la piste
Et le spectateur fou s'amuse
Au concert des Iles Marquises
                Le café clair
Elle est bien mise
Elle pose ses bijoux de verre
Et ses mains sont des écrevisses
La paille qu'elles prennent glisse
      Chapeau
                Bracelets
                        Faux linon
        La musique joue
Je voudrais bien sortir
            pour voir si le ciel est encore là

THE EXOTIC

An immortal profile on the pediment
In Borneo or beyond
            Frozen rivers
The animals race on the track
And the crazy spectator is entertained
At the concert in the Marquesas
                Bright café
She looks very stylish
Arranging her glass jewelry
Her hands are crayfish
The straw that they pick up slips
        Hat
            Bracelets
                    Fake batiste
        The music plays on
I'd like to get out of here
            to see if the sky is still there

ÉTOILE FILANTE

A la pointe où se balance un mouchoir blanc
          Au fond noir qui finit le monde
       Devant nos yeux un petit espace
                Tout ce qu'on ne voit pas
                   Et qui passe

       Le soleil donne un peu de feu

Une étoile filante brille
Et tout tombe
                Le ciel se ride
Les bras s'ouvrent
                   Et rien ne vient
Un cœur bat encore dans le vide

       Un soupir douloureux s'achève
Dans les plis du rideau le jour se lève

SHOOTING STAR

At the point where a white handkerchief sways
      On the black background closing the world
   A blankness in front of our eyes
         Everything we don't see
          That passes by

   A bit of fire from the sun

A shooting star gleams
And everything falls
           The sky is creased
Arms open wide
       And nothing comes
A heart beats on in the empty space

   A painful sigh dies out
In the folds of the curtain dawns the day

SOMBRE

Une longue aiguille traverse le rond
Un arbre
                    Un doigt
              La lune borgne
Une fenêtre qui nous lorgne
          La maison fatiguée s'endort
Un appel bref au bord de l'eau
L'argent coule le long des arbres
Ta figure est un bloc de marbre
Où sont passés tous les oiseaux
          La nuit
                    Le bruit
      Quelqu'un fait signe de se taire

On marche dans l'allée du petit cimetière

DARK

A long needle crosses the circle
A tree
                          A finger
            The one-eyed moon
A monocle-window aimed at us
            The tired house goes to sleep
A brief summons from the water's edge
Along the trees flows silver
Featureless marble your face
Where have the birds all gone
      Night
                                Noises
      A finger on someone's lips

On the path of the little cemetery footsteps

FAUSSE PORTE OU PORTRAIT

Dans la place qui reste là
Entre quatre lignes
          Un carré où le blanc se joue
      La main qui soutenait ta joue
                Lune
      Une figure qui s'allume
          Le profil d'un autre
                    Mais tes yeux
Je suis la lampe qui me guide
Un doigt sur la paupière humide
              Au milieu
      Les larmes roulent dans cet espace
                Entre quatre lignes
                Une glace

FALSE PORTAL OR PORTRAIT

        In this unmoving square
Inside four lines
            A space for the play of white
        The hand placed underneath your cheek
            The moon
        Lights up a face
            Another's profile
                But your eyes
I am the lamp to guide me
A finger on a moistened lid
            In the middle
        Tears are rolling through this space
                Inside four lines
                A mirror

VENDREDI TREIZE

La feuille vole cachant l'ombre
        Un jour de plus vient s'ajouter au nombre
Les passants arrêtés à l'étage au-dessus
        Quelqu'un descend
        L'araignée monte
Ou la cage de l'ascenseur
Un oiseau qui ne chante pas parce qu'il a peur
        Un enfant pleure et se résigne
Dans la maison où tout est noir
        Sous la marque du triste signe
Et sur le champ bordé d'espoir
La lumière monte et décline

        Un vœu trop lourd pour le hasard
S'est échappé de ma poitrine

FRIDAY THE THIRTEENTH

The shadow hidden by a leaf in flight
      The total is increased by one day more
The passersby who stopped on the upper floor
      Someone goes down
      The spider up
Or the elevator cage
A bird who isn't singing out of fright
      A crying child gives up its protest
In the house that's all dark
      And marked by the sign of sorrow
On the field bounded by hope
Light rises and declines

      Too heavy for luck a wish
Escaped from my breast

CLARTÉS TERRESTRES

Et encore une autre lumière
Le nombre en augmente toujours
Autant d'étoiles que de jours
                    J'attends
Que passe là derrière
La voix qui monte la première
                    Le monde regarde à son tour
Le soleil pourrait disparaître
Un astre nouveau vient de naître
                    Eclairant le ciel
Un œil immense artificiel
Qui regarde passer les autres
Avec plus de curiosité
Sur le visage inquiet qui change
                    Un éclair d'électricité

TERRESTRIAL CLARITIES

And still another light
The number is endlessly increased
As many stars as days
                    I wait
For there to be passing behind
The voice that is the first to rise
                    The world in its turn observes
The sun could disappear
A new star born just now
                    Illuminates the sky
An immense artificial eye
Watching the others pass by
With more curiosity
On its worried changing face
                    A flash of electricity

DANS LES CHAMPS OU SUR LA COLLINE

Non
              Le personnage historique
Et là le soleil s'arrêtait
C'était un homme qui passait
              Le cheval si maigre
              Qu'aucune ombre ne poursuivait

La neige serait étonnante
              Tout était blanc à quelques pas

Sur tous les animaux qui moururent de froid
              Entre les arbres et la mer
L'eau clapotante
                       Le ciel amer
    Resté seul entre les paysans et la lune
Le soir qui descendait devait venir de loin
Lentement la chanson dépassait nos mémoires
                       Fallait-il sourire ou y croire
       On attendait
                       On regardait
C'est à tout ce qui se passait ailleurs que l'on pensait

IN THE FIELDS OR ON THE HILL

                No
                Historical figure
And there the sun was coming to a stop
It was a man passing by
                His horse so thin
                Not the slightest shadow followed

The snow would be astonishing
                A few steps away and everything was white

Over all the animals who died of cold
                Between the trees and the sea
Quick lapping water
                The bitter sky
    Left alone between the peasants and the moon
The evening was coming down and from far away
Slowly the song was leaving our memories behind
                Were we supposed to smile or believe it
        We were waiting
                And watching
Everything happening elsewhere was in our minds

See note

SURPRISE

Dans la ville il n'y a plus personne
On monte à travers les bois
Quelques-uns tombent
       Et ceux qui arriveront trop tard
C'est toi
              C'est moi
La cheminée fume derrière
  Il est resté couché en bas
       Et toi tu t'agenouilles pour toujours
Il a la tête et le cœur lourds
  Et la chanson est oubliée
         Les heures que l'on a sautées
           A dormir les yeux ouverts
Ne regarde pas ce tableau
C'est une glace brisée
Et ton œil
  ton œil qui n'a pas encore l'habitude

SURPRISE

There is no one left in the city
Climbing up through the woods
A few fall down
       And those who will get there too late
You
             And I
Smoke from the chimney behind
  He is still lying there at the bottom
       And you go down on your knees forever
His head and his heart are heavy
  And the song forgotten
            The hours that we skipped over
           Asleep with open eyes
Don't look at this picture
It's a broken mirror
And your eyes
    your eyes aren't used to it yet

CALME INTÉRIEUR

Tout est calme
Pendant l'hiver
Au soir quand la lampe s'allume
A travers la fenêtre où on la voit courir
Sur le tapis des mains qui dansent
Une ombre au plafond se balance
On parle plus bas pour finir
Au jardin les arbres sont morts
Le feu brille
Et quelqu'un s'endort
Des lumières contre le mur
Sur la terre une feuille glisse
La nuit c'est le nouveau décor
Des drames sans témoin qui se passent dehors

THE PEACEFULNESS INSIDE

It's all so peaceful
During the winter
     In the evening when the lamp lights up
  Through the window we see it racing
Over the tablecloth dancing hands
On the ceiling a swaying shadow
    Our voices are lower now
In the garden the trees are dead
The fire sparkles
     And someone falls asleep
  Lights play on the wall
A sliding leaf on the ground
  The setting has changed to night
For disasters no one sees going on outside

SENTIER

Le vent trop fort ferme ma porte
Emporte mon chapeau comme une feuille morte
Tout a disparu dans la poussière
    Qui sait ce qu'il y a par derrière

Un homme court sur l'horizon
Son ombre tombe dans le vide
Les nuages plus lourds roulent sur la maison
    Le front du ciel inquiet se ride
Il y a des signes clairs au fer de l'occident
Une étoile qui tremble entre les fils d'argent
Les plis de la rivière qui arrêtera tout
Le monde fatigué s'affaisse dans un trou
    Et du massacre ce qui reste
Se dresse dans la nuit qui change tous les gestes

PATH

Too strong a wind shuts my door
Takes off with my hat like a dead leaf
All is lost in the dust
    Who knows what there is behind

A man runs along the horizon
His shadow falls into empty space
The heavier clouds go rolling over the house
    The worried sky wrinkled its brow
There are clear signs in the iron of the west
A trembling star between the silver threads
Folds of the river to make an end of it all
The weary world sinks deep into a hollow
    And what of the massacre remains
Rises up in the night when every gesture changes

MATINÉE

L'ombre penche plutôt à droite
Sous l'or qui luit
Dans le ciel qui fait mille plis
L'air bleu
                  Une étoffe irréelle
C'est peut-être une autre dentelle
A la fenêtre
          Qui bat comme une paupière
A cause du vent
     L'air
              Le soleil
                       L'été
Les traits de la saison sont à peine effacés

MORNING

The shadow leans more to the right
Under the gold gleaming
In a thousand pleats of the sky
The air is blue
                        Unheard-of fabric
Perhaps a new kind of lace
At the window
                Beating like an eyelid
Because of the wind
        The air
                    The sun
                            Summer
The season's features have scarcely been erased

MONTRE

Alors sur le soleil midi devait sonner
                    Sur cet immense gong
Un poing lourd s'abattait
Aux applaudissements de tous

Personne n'est resté couché

Les rayons sont déjà debout dans les allées
                    Au-dessus de chacun une blanche figure
Tout est noyé dans l'air dans la verdure
Mais quand le soir s'est rallumé
La porte était trop basse
                    Et le corps fatigué
Il a fallu traîner son ombre
                    Le boîtier s'était refermé
On y lisait un autre nombre
La lune au quart de nuit s'était mise à veiller

WATCH

Then on the sun was to fall the stroke of noon
                                   On that enormous gong
A heavy fist striking down
Applauded by all

No one has stayed in bed

The light rays are already upright on the paths
                    A white face over each one
And everything drowned in the air in foliage
But when evening lit up again
The door was too low
                    And the tired body
Had to drag its shadow along
                    The watchcase was closed
And there was a different number
The moon on guard at night had begun its vigil

COULOIR

Nous sommes deux
     Sur la même ligne où tout se suit
     Dans les méandres de la nuit
Une parole est au milieu
     Deux bouches qui ne se voient pas
     Un bruit de pas
Un corps léger glisse vers l'autre
          La porte tremble
Une main passe
    On voudrait ouvrir
    Le rayon clair se tient debout
    Là devant moi
    Et c'est le feu qui nous sépare
Dans l'ombre où ton profil s'égare
    Une minute sans respirer
Ton souffle en passant m'a brûlé

CORRIDOR

There are two of us
        On the same line where everything follows
        In night's winding ways
Surrounding a word
        The blindness of two mouths
        A sound of footsteps
One weightless body sliding toward the other
                                The door trembles
A passing hand
        Why not open
        The ray of clear light stands upright
        Before my eyes
                And it's the fire that comes between us
In the shadow where your profile wanders away
        For a moment not drawing a breath
Yours going by has burned me

VISITE

Les bateaux s'étageaient dans le tableau du fond
Où les hommes jouaient aux cartes
Les mots les plus légers montent jusqu'au plafond
Devant eux la fumée s'écarte
Les autres battent des ailes dans les plis des rideaux
L'ennui de la soirée pèse sur les cerveaux
Un livre a refermé ses portes
La prison des pensées où la mienne était morte
Toutes les bouches qui riront
Gagneront la fenêtre et l'air sur le balcon
Les vitres d'en face pâlissent
Dehors tout l'univers résonne
L'heure est venue
                    La cloche sonne
Et tous deux nous nous regardions
Perdus entre les murs de la même maison

VISIT

The boats were stacked in the picture on the wall
Where the men were playing cards
The lightest words rise all the way to the ceiling
Pushing aside the smoke
The others beat their wings in the curtains' folds
The evening's tedium weighs down our brains
A book has closed its doors
Prison of thoughts my own lies dead in there
All of the laughing mouths
Will reach the window the balcony fresh air
The windowpanes across the way grow pale
Outside the resonance of the universe
The hour has come
                    At the sound of the bell
The two of us were looking at each other
Lost inside the walls of the same house

COUVRE-FEU

Un coin au bout du monde où l'on est à l'abri
Les colonnes du soir se tendent
Et la porte s'ouvre à la nuit
Une seule lampe qui veille
Au fond il y a une merveille
Des têtes qu'on ne connaît pas
Au mur des plans qui se ressemblent
Ma figure plus effacée
Entre nous deux l'air chaud qui tremble
      Un souvenir détérioré
Entre les quatre murs qui craquent
    Personne ne parle
Le feu s'éteint sous la fumée

CURFEW

A place of refuge at the end of the world
The pillars of evening reach out
And the door stands open for night
Only one lamp keeps vigil
In the background the wonder
Of unfamiliar faces
The maps on the wall look alike
My own features more effaced
Between the two of us warm trembling air
     A disintegrated memory
Closed inside creaking walls
   No one talks
Smoke smothers the fire

ENTRE DEUX MONDES

L'ombre danse
Il n'y a plus rien
Que le vent qui s'élance
Le mouvement s'étend du mur
Et se gonfle
Il y a des personnages qui naissent
Pour une minute ou pour l'Eternité
La nuit seule qui change
Et moi-même à côté
Quelqu'un que le remords tracasse
Sur la route où marque son pas
On ne voit rien de ce qu'il y a
Le mur seul fait une grimace
Un signe de mon cœur s'étend jusqu'à la mer
Personne d'assez grand pour arrêter la terre
Et ce mouvement qui nous lasse
Quand une étoile bleue là-haut tourne à l'envers

BETWEEN TWO WORLDS

Dancing shadow
And nothing at all
But the spring of the wind
The movement reaches out from the wall
To grow
Some fictions come to life
For a moment or for Eternity
All that changes is night
And I close by
Someone plagued by remorse
On a route where his footsteps leave a trace
What is there we never see
Only the wall makes a face
My heart's gesture reaches out to the sea
Who's big enough to bring the world to a stop
And that movement which makes us weary
When a blue star up there turns in reverse

See note

VUE D'AUTREFOIS

La cloche qui sonnait au loin
                              Dès le réveil
Battement d'aile
                    Sur ma tête où joue le soleil
Un souvenir remue à peine
                    Mon cœur s'arrête d'écouter
              Les voix qui parlent
Depuis longtemps tout ce qui s'est passé
Est-ce le même
                    En passant qui m'a regardé

Ce sont les mêmes yeux qui tournent
                              Mais le portrait s'est effacé

Les traits de ton visage s'écartent
                              Un autre vient
Le front vieilli qu'avait caché ta main
Enfin la voix qui parle
                    Un enfant qui courait ne te rappelle rien
Et celui qui s'en va là-bas
                              Tes lèvres tremblent
Dans un pays lointain et noir
                    Tu lui ressembles

A VIEW FROM LONG AGO

The bell tolling from far away
                          As soon as I was awake
A beating of wings
                 On my head where the sunlight plays
A memory scarcely stirs
                 My heart stops hearing
             The voices talking
For so long was all that has come to pass
The same
                 Passing by with a look at me

Those are the same eyes moving
                 But the portrait is effaced

Your features leave their place
                 To others
From underneath your hand the aging forehead
And finally your voice
                 That running child evokes no memory
There's another in the distance moving away
                 Your lips tremble
Through a country remote and dark
                 you resemble

See note

CHAMBRE NOIRE

Un trou dans la lumière et la porte l'encadre
Tout est noir
Les yeux se sont remplis d'un sombre désespoir
                    On rit
Mais la mort passe
              Dans son écharpe ténébreuse
              Et dans le sillon creux
                              Une bête peureuse
Qui se débat pour fuir
Vers le fond du jardin où la porte est ouverte
Mais — quelqu'un vient d'entrer
Sans oser dire un mot
La lune est toute gonflée d'eau
Dans la nuit les nuages montent
J'attends l'heure qui sonne
Et je peux écouter
La fin d'un autre conte

DARKROOM

A hole in the light that the door encloses
Everything's dark
The eyes have filled up with a somber despair
                    Someone laughs
But death passes by
                    In his shadowy scarf
                    And within the hollow furrow
                                        A timid creature
Struggling to flee
Through the garden toward an open door
But — someone just came in
Not daring to say anything
Water has swollen the moon
Through the night move clouds ascending
I await the striking hour
And I can listen
To another story's ending

See note

CAMPAGNE

Le champ s'incline à la lumière
Au bas du ciel bleu plus serein
La route court sous la poussière
Mais le soleil n'y est pour rien

La voix qui monte est sans éclat
Un gai refrain dans la voiture
Qui file à l'horizon plus plat
Sur les roues d'or dans la verdure
Un pan de mur blanc s'élargit
Sous mes yeux qui tournent la meule
Un dernier rayon s'étourdit
Sur le cuivre des tiges molles

Le jour s'est écrasé derrière la maison
Il n'y a plus qu'un trou sous la lampe
Les soucis écartés et même notre espoir
Qui descend plus vite la rampe
Quand la fenêtre allume un feu neuf dans le soir

COUNTRYSIDE

The field bows to the light
Below the more serene blue sky
Deep in dust the wide road runs
But none of it concerns the sun

The rising voice is lusterless
A gay refrain in the carriage
Rushing along the flatter horizon
On golden wheels through the foliage
Part of a white wall extends
Before my eyes turning the millstone
A last ray of light grows dizzy
On coppery and yielding stems

The day has crashed behind the house
All that's left is a hole under the lamp
The worries set aside and our hope as well
Going more quickly down the ramp
When the window lights up a new fire at nightfall

PATIENCE

Les voix qui s'élevaient tremblent à l'horizon
Tout est calme dans la clairière
On pourrait voir passer ceux qui s'en vont
Sur cette route sans ornières
D'où vient celui que l'on ne connaît pas
A l'intérieur les gens regardent
Les mains plus vivantes qui passent
Sur celles que l'on ne voit pas
Les mots sont plus lourds que le son
   Ils tombent
Les paupières battent
    On a parlé bas sur ce ton
Et un astre nouveau s'élève
L'espoir luit
    Une porte bouge
     L'arbre d'en face s'est penché
Le mur s'allonge infiniment
     Il n'y a rien de clair dans ma tête
      Sur le trottoir noir et luisant
Toujours le même qui s'arrête

PATIENCE

The voices that were rising tremble on the horizon
All is peaceful in the clearing
A place from which to see those disappearing
Along the rutless road
Whence comes the person we don't know
They are watching from inside
The livelier hands passing over
The ones that can't be seen
Words are heavier than sound
       They fall down
The eyelids flutter
       There was quiet speech in that tone of voice
And a new star rises
Hope shines
       A door makes a move
       Across the way a tree bends closer
The wall endlessly lengthens
       Nothing is clear inside my head
         On the black and shining sidewalk
The same one stops every time

VISAGE

Il sait à peine d'où tu viens
Malgré la ride qui te marque
Malgré ces traces sur tes joues
Et les mouvements de tes mains
Il ne veut pas que tu t'en ailles
Sur la chaise il n'y a plus qu'un trou
Une forme vague dans l'ombre
Le portrait au fusain dans le coin le plus sombre
Presque rien
Sur le mur quelqu'un passe sa main
Dans les volets le vent se fâche
Tout est fermé jusqu'au matin
Lui doit être loin sur la route

FACE

He scarcely knows where you come from
Despite the wrinkle that brands you
And those lines on your cheeks
And the way your hands move
He doesn't want you to go away
All that's left in the chair is a hole
An indistinct form in the shadow
The charcoal portrait in the darkest corner
Almost nothing
Someone passes his hand over the wall
In the shutters the wind rages
Everything's closed until morning
He must be well on his way by now

CORTÈGE

Les mains dressées plus haut touchaient presque le
    toit
Plus loin les yeux se ferment sur tout ce que l'on voit
La lune au cou tordu les bras sont accrochés
Les arbres sous le vent se hâtent de marcher
Au timbre de ta voix le ciel tiède se vide
Les étoiles perdues tombent dans le ruisseau
Et sur ta main des perles brillent
Pourtant la pluie ne tombe pas
On éteint toutes les fenêtres
Les nuages volent plus bas
La rue se ferme à la tempête
A tous les coups qu'on n'entend pas
Quand le dernier venu franchit la porte basse
C'est derrière le mur le plus épais que tout se passe

PROCESSION

The hands raised higher were almost touching the roof
Further on eyes close to all that can be seen
The moon has a twisted neck arms hanging on
Making haste beneath the wind go trees
The sound of your voice empties the warm sky
The lost stars are falling into the stream
And on your hand pearls glow
Yet the rain does not fall
They turn off all the windows
The clouds fly nearer the ground
The street is closed to the storm
To all the inaudible blows
When the last to arrive gets through the low door
It's behind the thickest wall that everything happens

.

PROJETS

Où iront-ils chercher tout ce qu'il y a
            de grave derrière leurs têtes
Le ciel plisse son front
                    Prépare une tempête
Les autres sont là pour la fête
Et les astres tendent des fils
De maison à maison
            Les ondes des clochers ébranlent la cloison
Tout est triste plus loin
Et même leurs chansons
            Les hommes fatigués s'étirent
Au jour les lumières pâlissent
  Et sur le trottoir mouillé glissent
            Tous leurs désirs éparpillés
Qui restent morts dans la coulisse
De l'ombre épaisse où ils sont nés

PLANS

Where will they look for everything
                that counts in the back of their heads
The sky wrinkles its brow
                        Gets a storm ready
The others are there to celebrate
And the stars are stringing threads
From house to house
                The partition rocks under waves from the carillon
It's all sad farther on
And even their songs
                Tired men are stretching
In the daylight lamps grow pale
   And over the wet pavement glide
                All their scattered desires
In the wings behind the depths of shadow
Where they were born they lie dead now

COURSE

On peut regarder de travers
Tous ceux qui passent sous l'averse
Les voix qui criaient à l'envers
Et les animaux en détresse
A peine relevés du ciel
Sous les têtes tranchées aux lames des rayons
Quand le soleil fond sur les larmes
Que les yeux perdent leur aplomb
Dans les yeux qu'ils regardent
La chute au fond de la raison
Le tonnerre des voix qui grondent
Sous la voûte éclatante où s'engouffre le monde
La terre était pleine de trous
Le ciel restait toujours limpide
Et les mains cherchaient dans le vide
L'horizon qui n'existe pas

RACING

One may have one's doubts about
Everyone passing by beneath the downpour
The voices that were crying in reverse
And the animals in distress
Only just now helped up from the sky
Under the heads cut off by blades of light
When the sun hurls itself against tears
And the eyes drop their assurance
Into the eyes they meet
The fall to the depths of reason
The thunder of scolding voices
Beneath the dazzling dome which engulfs the world
The ground was full of holes
The sky was still clear
And hands were searching the emptiness
For the non-existent horizon

ÉTAPE

Le cavalier mourant levait pourtant sa tête
    Les étoiles le fusillaient
La haie du rêve noir est encore trop épaisse
Nous ne sortirons pas du sort des prisonniers
Mais on peut voir déjà ce qui se passe
Dans les maisons ou sur les toits
Et l'immense bloc où s'entassent
    Mêmes les hommes qui sont là
Les animaux suivent en tas
    La route aux vagues de poussière
Le fleuve où les reflets se noient
    Et les souvenirs qui se meuvent
Dans l'univers refait qui tourne devant toi
    Dans une minute rapide
L'arbre d'en face s'est brisé
Le talus grimpe sur la rive
        Tout le monde s'est incliné
Il faut aller plus lentement
        A cause des plans qui se croisent
        A cause des enterrements
        Et des réveils qui nous déçoivent
        Sous les larmes du firmament

STOPPING PLACE

The dying horseman managed to raise his head
    Under the fusillade from the stars
The black hedge of dream is still too thick
Whatever happens to captives will happen to us
But already we can see what's being done
In the houses or on the roofs
And piling up on that enormous block
    Even the men who are there
The piles of animals follow
    The wide road with its waves of dust
The river of drowning reflections
    The memories stirring
In the newborn universe turning before your eyes
    In a swift moment
The tree over there has broken
The bank climbs up the shore
      Everyone has bowed
We have to proceed more slowly
        Because of the projects that intersect
        Because of the open graves
        And the disappointment when we open our eyes
        Under the tears of the sky

ÉCRAN

Une ombre coule sur ta main
La lampe a changé ta figure
La pendule bat
                    Le temps dure
Et comme il ne se passe rien
Celui qui regardait s'en va
                    Le monde se retourne et rit
Pour regarder tout ce qui vit

                    On marche encore dans le doute
Un tournant au bout de la route
                    Une forêt
Un pont sans arches
                    Et la maison où je vivrais
Il faut partir coûte que coûte
Et l'ombre qui passait
                    Celui qui regardait
Le monde qui riait
                    S'évanouissent
Au fond contre le mur
                    Des silhouettes glissent

SCREEN

Over your hand flows a shadow
The lamp has altered your face
The clock is ticking
                    Time remains
And since nothing else is happening
The spectator goes his way
                    The world turns around and laughs
To see all that's alive

                    We go onward still uncertain
At the end of the road there's a turn
                    A forest
A simple bridge
                    And the house where I'd like to live
We must leave just the same
And the passing shadow
                    The man who was looking on
The laughing world
                    Subside
In the background on the wall
                    Silhouettes glide

ET LA

Quelqu'un parle et je suis debout
Je vais partir là-bas à l'autre bout
         Les arbres pleurent
Parce qu'au loin d'autres choses meurent
            Maintenant la tête a tout pris

Mais je ne t'ai pas encore compris
Je marche sur tes pas sans savoir qui je suis
Il faut passer par une porte où personne n'attend
        Pour un impossible repos
  Tout s'écarte et montre le dos
          Un peu de vide reste autour
Et pour revivre d'anciens jours
Une âme détachée s'amuse
Et traîne encore un corps qui s'use
Le dernier temps d'une mesure
Plus tenace et plus déchirant
Un chagrin musical murmure

AND THERE

Someone is talking and here I stand
I'm going to move down there to the other end
          The trees are crying
Because in the distance other things are dying
             Now the head has taken it all

But I haven't understood you yet
Wondering who I can be I walk in your footsteps
There is a door to pass where no one waits
          For an impossible lull
   Everything turns its back as it moves aside
            Where a little emptiness stays
And to relive long-lost days
A soul in its detachment plays
Dragging around its worn-out flesh again
Through the last beats of a measure
More heart-rending more tenacious
Murmurs a musical distress

LA SAISON DERNIÈRE

Un regard
                ou une grimace
        Le soleil a lui
Dans le miroir ce n'est plus le même
                Un nuage passe à cheval
        En courant le vent le dépasse
Une ombre sur l'œil me tracasse
        Je glisse dans un cauchemar

                Un masque noir
                        souligné d'un sourire
                Et celui qui m'entraîne crie
                Il pourrait être mieux ou pire
                        et je ris

        Dans la cour il n'y a que moi
    Un manteau sombre flotte au-dessus du toit
                Plein de trous
                        et quelqu'un m'appelle
    Ma paupière est frôlée par un vol d'hirondelles
    C'est une main gantée
                Le reste passe derrière les souvenirs
        Mais ce qui est là je pourrais le tenir

Si tu ne regardais pas toujours en arrière

LAST SEASON

Did someone look
             or make a face
     The sun lit up
It's another scene in the mirror
              A cloud on horseback passes by
          The wind rushes to win the race
I'm annoyed by a shadow in my eye
             And slip into nightmare

            A black mask
              a smile underlines
        And dragging me off someone cries
       It could be better or worse
             to my laughter

    I'm all alone in the courtyard
Above the roof a dark coat floats
              Full of holes
               and someone is calling me

My eyelid is brushed by a swallow's wing
It's a hand in a glove
            The rest passes behind the memories
    But what's there I could keep hold of

If you weren't always looking back

EN BAS

L'éclair passe à travers la bague
Le diamant reste à ton doigt
    La ligne sortait du coin le plus sombre
Celle qui était à son bras formée de l'ombre
avait changé
                La femme souriait
Sous quel jeu de lumière
                    La pièce est-elle transformée
Le plafond reste noir
               Voyez sur le balcon
Aujourd'hui les étoiles marchent
                 On fait semblant de ne pas voir
Parfois les yeux aussi se lèvent
                 Pas si haut
  On pourrait tomber
Le vent qui charge aura tout emporté
Il ne reste plus que la terre
Et ceux qui n'ont pas pu monter

DOWN BELOW

The flash of lightning passes through the ring
The diamond stays on your finger
     The line was coming out of the darkest corner
The one shadow formed on his arm
had changed
       The woman was smiling
Thanks to what play of light
        Has the room been transformed
The ceiling is still dark
      Look on the balcony
The stars are on the march today
       We pretend not to see
Sometimes our eyes rise too
       Not so high
  We might fall
The charging wind must have carried it all away
Except for the earth
And those who failed in the climb

TÊTE

Nous ne sommes plus là
                    Les autres sont venus
                         Pendant la nuit
Je suis derrière
               Les visages que j'ai connus
Entre les cheminées qui mangent la lumière
Le ciel a grimacé
               Un front soucieux s'est montré

Pendant que nous étions en fête
          Et l'on voyait tourner toutes les têtes
               Que le rire fait éclater
Une lampe s'est allumée
Dans la maison qui ouvre ses fenêtres
Les yeux se sont mis à briller
        Les éclats se brisaient en tombant dans la rue

Et les voix s'élevaient que l'on a entendues
A celle qui restait j'aurais mêlé la mienne
Mais tes yeux se sont refermés
                    Et même les persiennes
                         Sont retombées

HEAD

We aren't there any more
                    The others came
                    During the night
I am behind
          The faces I have known
Between the chimneys eating up the light
A grimace from the sky
          An anxious forehead appeared

While we were having fun
          And all the heads that laughter
                    Bursts were seen to turn
A lamp went on
As the house opens its windows
Suddenly sparkling eyes
          The scintillations broke as they fell on the street

And the voices we heard began to rise
Except for the one to which I'd have added mine
But once again you've closed your eyes
                    And even the blinds
                              Have rolled down

AVANT L'HEURE

Elle est allumée
On ne voit plus qu'elle
   Et le cœur triangulaire
    Qui brille au soleil
Une matinée
Une aube nouvelle
    Mais la journée amère
     Qui reste pareille
Salué en passant quelques yeux inconnus
Où passe le regard que chacun emporte
Et le nom que l'on a cloué
Sur chacune des deux portes
J'ai crié en frappant
     On ne répondait pas
J'ai pleuré en partant
     Mais sans qu'aucun me voie
Et toute la tristesse est restée enfermée
Attendant le soleil qui ouvre les fenêtres
Et les desseins obscurs qui roulent dans ma tête

BEFORE THE HOUR

All lit up
All anyone can see
      Plus the triangular heart
      Shining in the sun
The new start
Of a morning
      The bitter part
      It's the same old day
Having greeted in passing a few unknown eyes
And the look that passed each one would carry away
With the name they nailed
On both of the doors
I shouted as I knocked
      No one replied
As I left I cried
      But no one could have known
And all the sadness has stayed inside
Waiting for the sun to open the windows
And the shadowy projects rolling around in my mind

MÉMOIRE

Une minute à peine
                    Et je suis revenu
De tout ce qui passait je n'ai rien retenu
Un point
            Le ciel grandi
                        Et au dernier moment
La lanterne qui passe
                    Le pas que l'on entend
    Quelqu'un s'arrête entre tout ce qui marche
On laisse aller le monde
                        Et ce qu'il y a dedans
Les lumières qui dansent
                        Et l'ombre qui s'étend
Il y a plus d'espace
                        En regardant devant
Une cage où bondit un animal vivant
La poitrine et les bras faisaient le même geste
Une femme riait
                    En renversant la tête
Et celui qui venait nous avait confondus
Nous étions tous les trois sans nous connaître
Et nous formions déjà
                        Un monde plein d'espoir

MEMORY

Scarcely a minute
Before I've come back
Having grasped nothing of all that passed
One point
      The larger sky
           And at the last moment
The lantern going by
         The footstep overheard
  Of all that's in motion someone comes to a stop
Let the world go on as it will
        And everything in it
The dancing lights
        And the spreading shadow
There's more space
        Looking straight ahead
Inside a cage a living animal leaped
With an identical gesture of breast and arms
A woman laughed
       Throwing back her head
And someone mistook the one of us for the other
All three of us were strangers
And formed already
       A world full of hope

BARRE D'AZUR

Les débris culbutés dans le coin
       Il ne reste plus rien
              Les murs et le triangle
Pourtant
     L'espoir qui nous soutient
L'objet que l'on tient dans la main
  Il fait jour
          Et l'on marche mieux
La rue est plafonnée de bleu
       Et nos projets sont sans limite
On ne voit pas passer le temps
        Qui va plus vite
          Dans l'air

Sans savoir si l'on tourne à droite
        Ou à l'envers

A BAR OF AZURE

Debris kicked into a corner
        Nothing remains
                The triangle and the walls
Yet
    Hope sustains us
An object to hold in the hand
    Daylight
             And we walk more easily
The street has a blue ceiling
          And we have no end of plans
We don't see the time passing by
        It goes faster
           In the air

Not knowing if we're to turn right
        Or in reverse

NUIT

Derrière la porte où je suis caché
Le soir tarde à venir

Je regarde le ciel par cet œil en losange

Minuit

Les avions de feu sont presque tous passés
A travers les signaux d'alarme

Il y avait dans ma poche une arme

Une aile qui battait moins haut

La lune retenant ses larmes

Et des rires moqueurs dans les plis du rideau

NIGHT

In my hiding place behind the door
Evening is slow in coming

Through this diamond-shaped eye there's the sky

Midnight

Almost all the warplanes went by
Straight through the alarm

In my pocket I had a firearm

A wing beating now not so high

Tears that the moon withholds

And mocking laughter in the curtain's folds

REGARD

Assis sur l'horizon
Les autres vont chanter
Et nous nous avons regardé
La voiture en passant souleva
la poussière
Et tout ce qui traînait retomba
par derrière
Mon œil suivait ainsi
la ligne des ornières
Il s'étirait sans en souffrir
Ton regard le faisait rougir
Et cette voix qui pleure
Sans soulever un souvenir
Est devenue meilleure
Il n'y a plus rien que ton regard
Et devant toi tous ceux qui t'offensèrent

A LOOK

                    Seated on the horizon
                The others are going to sing
And as for us we looked on
                    The carriage passing by thrust upward
                    the dust
                    And all that trailed
                    fell back down
                My eye following thus
                            the line of rust
                    Stretched out painlessly
                    Your look was making it blush
And that voice full of sorrow
    Not stirring the dust on the past
    Is better now
                        And there is nothing left but the look in your eyes
        Facing all those you have reasons to distrust

See note

Notes to The Roof Slates

P. 23. The title "Hawking" is intended to suggest the two meanings of *réclame;* The call that summons a hunting bird back to the lure, and a flamboyant advertisement.

P. 27. *sur le champ:* immediately, and literally, on the field. *la barrière:* one of the many barriers, and one of the few to be crossed, at whatever cost. Cf. pp. 41, 49.

P. 33. "on pourrait mourir": *on* includes poet and reader, everyone; it is impersonal and yet familiar. The line is repeated in "Sentinel," p. 83. The words rise like the prayers in the preceding poem, and also like bubbles filled with the breath of life. Elsewhere, songs and voices also rise.

P. 37. The title, "Abat-jour": a lampshade, but, literally, to strike down the day.

Rizzuto (*Style and Theme in Reverdy's Les Ardoises du Toit*, The University of Alabama Press, 1971) interprets this domestic scene as a lost paradise, but the narrator wants to leave, and the lips only "seem" pious.

P. 45. "m'atteindre": whether "they" would come to help or to harm is uncertain.

P. 49. *Noir* is variously translated in this book; it is lighter than black, darker than dark.

P. 65. "Mais qui dans la nuit est entré": *qui* is both a question and a condensed form of *celui qui* or *qui que ce soit qui,* meaning "whoever has . . ."
dans has the effect of *within.* One is inside of Reverdy's night with its closed door.

P. 75. "Leaden" in line 9 takes "sombre" to include its verbal meaning: to sink down.

P. 79. The identity of those who want to "come down" is less certain than it appears, because *quelques-uns* (a few of them) is masculine, and cannot refer to "stars."

P. 89. "We could see the light / Coming / We were happy . . ." This rare affirmation deserves to be noted.

P. 91. The last three lines in the 1918 version read:

> Quelque chose passe
> Un léger bruit
> Qui se cache

> Something passes by
> A slight noise
> Going to hide

P. 111. The rhyme *mer-amer* unites the sea and the sky.

P. 129. *le mouvement;* cf. "Marche forcée" in *Poèmes en prose*, 1915: "Mais va, le mouvement, le mouvement, et pour le repos ta fatigue."

The *vers* (verse) in *à l'envers* (in the wrong direction) is not to be neglected. Cf. p. 163 where it also occurs as the last word, and p. 145.

P. 131. The last line reads "You resemble it," hence the lower-case "you" in the English.

P. 133. In the place of death in a shadowy scarf, the 1918 version reads: "Irréalité lumineuse" (Luminous unreality).

P. 167. The verb *soulever* unites the rising dust and the possible rise of memories, literally, "not lifting upward a memory." This negative accomplishment also accounts for the voice's being "better." It is in the domain of art, not that of life.

Some Prose Poems

translated by
Mary Ann Caws

Real poetry is a gesture that counts.
(This Emotion Called Poetry)

Choice and Metapoetic

The subjects treated in this range of prose poems are few; they have been simply and openly chosen according to a subjective taste, but in the belief that they are also representative. They are situated in a certain landscape that we come to recognize, and that will not easily be forgotten, composed as it is of certain highly charged images and figures, traversed as it is by certain lines and strokes. These meditations on the poetic self, highly aware of its own creative oddness and its own peculiar genius, choose their setting and, on the whole, construct it as surroundings for the self. Regardless of the date of the text, this self is unmistakable: many of the poems, from early to late, illustrate above all an exacerbated reticence, as in the title given to one of the *Prose Poems* of 1915: "Timidity." It seems only fitting that such a

narrator should have his hat knocked off by the wind . . . But
the extraordinarily acute perception of the stranger aspects of the
lonely mind and of the obsessions governing it account for many
of the less common aspects of Reverdy's style.

May not, in fact, the hypertense *trouble* of the underlying
text as it clashes with the calmer surface — that surface that
keeps a very low profile — be considered to depend on precisely
this oddity of personality? May not, moreover, what we would
unquestionably recognize as Reverdy's extraordinary poetic sen-
sitivity be intimately involved in his excruciating nervousness? I
think we might understand his as a nervous perception, which
should be celebrated as such, quite on the other side of the
famous "monotony." ("I may be boring," said André Breton,
"but Pierre Reverdy is still more boring than I am.") The
nuanced perception demanded of the reader is here *interior* to the
design and the structure of the poems, and what might have
appeared monotonous in them turns out — once seen from the
inside — to be full of differentiation, color, and contrast.

In the prose poems exactly these nuances are clear: a de-
velopment of the range and sort of interior perception is notice-
able within them, even in their titles, from the peculiarly neutral
titles of the *Prose Poems* (1915) and the *Some Poems* (1916) on to the
visions already framed by the title that gives the perspective from
which they look, these poems of the *Oval Attic-Window* (1916).
That this *Lucarne ovale* can just as well be a skylight as a dormer
or attic-window links the point of the viewer's vision, which is to
say, his viewpoint, also to *Les Ardoises du toit* and to the *Painted
Stars* (1921), even in some sense to the *Glass Puddles* (1929), since
these are all constructions made between the sky in its brilliance
and human vision or artifice: drops in the gutter of the roof, stars
caught in the mirror of a water as in a glass, or painted, quite
simply, upon a windowpane. And all these senses are held, too,
in the clear ambiguities of the sounds as of the sight. Held, then,
in a glass, as in the *Plein verre* or *Full Glass* of a collection of poems
from 1940, or in a mirror, that *verre* of the *Flaques de verre* where
the stillness of the puddles turns them into a capturing surface,
or then, within a verse, that *vers* echoing in all the titles of these
conscious poems about poetry. Metapoetic, they are undeniably
that: and yet their fresh quality as picture is maintained, as in the
later *Bois vert* or *Green Wood* (1946-49), where the same sound as
that capturing the glass, the mirror, and the poem, now brings
out the density of the fullest cluster of sense and sound, each

meaning triggering the reader's retrospective or prospective read-
ing of the others. An extensive experience facilitates this reac-
tion. On the other side of the crystalline imagery, the harshness
of *Ferraille* or *Scrap Iron* (1937) brings out the alternate intelli-
gence of the poet's *faire*, his making, in its alliance with the *fer* or
iron, replacing and yet echoing in its own rhyme the *verre/vert/
vers*. As if Reverdy were indeed obsessed with that rhyme, the
last collection of his poems, *The Freedom of the Seas (Liberté des
mers)* from 1959, retains the *-er*, the sea of the final syllable
holding in itself both the *verre* in its glassiness and the *fer* in its
construction.

Now if we consider that single case of triple and quadruple
meaning as the sound is charged with its multiplicity, and con-
sider also the frequency of this occurrence, each reader may
well wonder to what extent other interpretations should be
conjured up within the poems, whether or not Reverdy's inten-
tions are taken into account. He himself, in an essay of 1938,
semi-ironically called "To Have Done With Poetry," says the
following: "If poetry makes too many compromises with the ear,
it does not reach the mind — if it weighs on the mind, it has lost
all its wing-feathers. The ear is the keyhole opening onto the
heart" (*This Emotion*, p. 138). So both the glass (*verre*) and the line
(*vers*) and the freshness of the green (*vert*) may be included in the
mind, in its own opening upon the heart. The summit poem of
Flaques de verre is called, appropriately, "The Head Filled with
Beauty," and it links the lines or *vers* with the others beyond
them, to which it refers, in the built-in library of intertextual ref-
erences; the poet here addresses, as it were, the poetry directly,
and in an accumulating crescendo:

> You, gentleness and hatred — horizon chipped away, pure line of
> indifference and oblivion. You, this morning, totally alone, in
> order, calm, and universal revolution. You, diamond nail. You,
> purity, dazzling swivel of the ebb and flow of my thought in the
> lines of the world. (pp. 134-5)

Throughout these poems, what strikes the alerted reader
even more than the individual themes may well be the essentially
metapoetic quality of these texts, many of which refer mainly to
their own being as texts: thus the continued emphasis on win-
dows and doors, on frames and curtains and edges, rims of a
glass, the *bords* or borders of riverbanks or ravines, and the

distinctions between light and shadow, lamps and what they reflect upon. These images can all be seen, I think, as the indications of a particular interest in the devices through or by which vision is itself bordered: an oval holds a face, as in "Soul and Body Superposed," or a portrait is framed by a window, in a text called "The Word," or a stress is laid on the eyes themselves, noticeable in a great number of poems: "A Mediocre Appearance," "Civil," "Trips Too Long," "Another Face," "At the Moment of the Banquet," "Afternoon," "Outside," among others.

Of all the devices, the most emblematic or self-sufficient — needing no interpretation beyond itself — is perhaps that of the finger and the hands, to which attention is drawn over and over. In the poem "When One is Not of This World," whose title may already be seen as a distancing of the poet from those who are of another calling — whose hands would undoubtedly be less in evidence — fingers trace upon a tablecloth an undecipherable name in large black letters, whereas in the poems of the last collection fingers are flung to the ceiling at the same moment that a spider is seen to be busily and vainly spinning, giving the title "The Web" to the poem, whose own web neatly links one "useless" gesture to another. (The poem is reminiscent of an earlier one, where hands are outstretched under a lamp; in another of the poems in *The Freedom of the Seas*, "The Mind Outside," hands are once more stretched out under the lamp, and a pen scratches late across a page. Elsewhere, white hands flutter, and everywhere, the mind grapples with its own self-mockery and with "The Luck of Words," as if it were some card game whose images captured the Cubist eye, whose luck involved us all, and poetry. We have only to note how many of the texts are called by such titles: "The Poets," "The Word," "The Luck of Words," "Mirror of Ink," to support the easily supported hypothesis that words, hands, and eyes, are all dissociated from ordinary language, severed from the matter of ordinary bodies and visions — as in the image from "The Poets," with severed hands lit under the lamp. Stressed, exalted in their very separation, these few images are charged now with special significance, emblematized in the poetry centered upon itself. This is of course a widespread notion, but Reverdy's "Chambre noire," or darkroom, with its claustrophobic atmosphere, impressive to the reader, helps to create the illusion that the self-reference is in this case especially acute.

A Moody Line

In my head, lines, nothing but lines; if
only I could make some order of them.
(Strokes and Figures)

As for the ambiance of the poems, the figures betraying it are to
be read in their own context, and total submersion in Reverdy's
universe is preferable to occasional plunges to its depths. The
atmosphere tends toward the gloomy: after an exaltation of
action, the closure is often associated with deception. For exam-
ple, in "After the Ball," dancers spin about and then the lamps
are extinguished, so that the erstwhile dancer is alone in the cold,
leaving the impression that something is missing. The road is
often blocked ("Soul and Body Superposed"), the curtains are
often drawn to close off the poem at the end of a spectacle, or the
light goes out ("The Ridiculous Bodies of the Minds"), or the
day ends ("Light"); the fields are most probably devastated
("Flames"), the rain most probably icy, the wall soaked or dirt-
ied, the dress sodden, the sky gray, and the very air may well be
blue-black and sore, as in the title "The Bruised Air." Rugs are
discolored ("Carnival") as is the flag whose symbol seems to wear
off ("Battle"), a white glove is faded ("Brief Life") — in short, the
physical universe is usually leaden and the human, fatigued
("Reality of Shadows" and passim.). Thoughts will most likely
be "low" or "lowly"; a child is starving, soldiers are afflicted, like
poets, with nightmares.

But a mud puddle will suffice to capture the spectacle and
the light of a universe, here as in Rimbaud's "Drunken Boat" or
in the poetry of Yves Bonnefoy, where language serves in just
this manner:

> Les mots comme le ciel,
> Infini,
> Mais tout entier soudain dans la flaque brève.
> (The words like the sky,
> Infinite,
> But entire suddenly in the brief puddle.)
> *In the Threshold's Lure*

The *Glass Puddles*, then, are a mirror for poetic reflection: "To
Each His Share" explains how such a water is sufficient for a

strange fisherman-like poet, who will not, as does another fisherman, scoop gold pieces whose gleam will be extinguished in a closed basket — who will not content himself, then, with the reflection of mere wealth, but rather, will dangle the line into the stars themselves as they shine within the water, these illusions being the matter for real fishing, for real poets:

This water, having come from the sky, was filled with stars.

And the stars are no less real there than the diamonds caught in the gutter of the roof, the diamond nail caught in the glass of some great poem, like a painted star of the *Étoiles peintes;* for in that puddle there is to be found all the *Freedom of the Seas.*

Interior Perception and the Self of Poetry

— What was the major encounter of your life?
(question asked in 1934 for the journal Minotaure)
— The only one, capital and so obviously
necessary . . . that which I believe I had
with myself, which will never end.
(This Emotion, p. 175)

Nowhere are Reverdy's aesthetics better summed up than in the essays grouped under the title *This Emotion Called Poetry: Writings on Poetry 1930-1960*, with the invaluable notes and commentaries furnished, as for all the Flammarion editions, by Étienne-Alain Hubert: this is the collection whose ancestor is the volume of essays on art and poetry collected in *Nord-Sud: Self-Defense.* . . .
Here, as always, the poet's attitude is a self-sufficient one: "to create an aesthetic work made of one's own means, a particular emotion that the things of nature, in their own situation, are not able to provoke in man." The explicit goal is the augmentation of being that a poem expresses and maintains: the love of the real through the book is along Mallarmé's lines, and in his line of sight; toward the self, the self struggles, through a vocabulary deliberately narrowed and vision in its self-enforced closure, masking and shutting off. (Seen in this light, the ubiquitous references to masks and masking are part of a whole attitude and concern, and not just the bizarre obsession of some psychotic writer.)

This volume also, being only a translation and second hand representation, is limited by its words and by their weakness, and dependent on the sensitivity that it is our aim to develop, in spite of and because of the very closure of the "dark room" that Reverdy uses so often as the image of the development of poetry. The sensitivity is a quiet one. It is not here a question of Rimbaldian dazzle in illumination, of Mallarméan complexity in its exhilaration, or of the monumental subtlety and the subtle monumentality of René Char, but rather of some summit within the poetic being — some other "Head Filled with Beauty" of an almost imperceptible kind, visible in any case only after the reading of a great deal of this poetry. Toward this perception Reverdy's reader may move, conscious that Reverdy's own manner is already a refusal of flashiness or outward drama. This is, and here the reader must share Reverdy's own faith, a work with delayed action, an "Oeuvre à retardement" (*This Emotion*, p. 112), a work whose beauty and force are revealed

> very slowly, by successive generations and for eminently contradictory reasons, that is to say, works holding in their net enough mystery to be only with great difficulty accessible to the simple watchers of the present — in brief, those works including between their visible constitutive elements enough white space, enough margin, so that succeeding generations can come to deposit in them, never weakening or profoundly altering the purity and value of their original structure, as much and even more substance than they could have gotten themselves. For in a work which lasts without aging, which grows while it lasts, all those who claim to love it, to understand it, to comment upon it, to spread it by amplifying it with a legend, even one which deforms it most of the time, all these collaborate. (*This Emotion*, pp. 112-113)

The present work, which desires to be a faithful reflection of and upon Reverdy's own work, tries neither to spread a legend nor to make an extensive commentary, but simply to participate, insofar as possible, in its own interior sensitivity.

Mary Ann Caws

Georges Braque, "La Lampe," © by ADAGP, Paris, 1981 (courtesy of the Bibliothèque Littéraire Jacques Doucet).

Poems

FÉTICHE

Petite poupée, marionnette porte-bonheur, elle se débat à ma fenêtre, au gré du vent. La pluie a mouillé sa robe, sa figure et ses mains qui déteignent. Elle a même perdu une jambe. Mais sa bague reste, et, avec elle, son pouvoir. L'hiver elle frappe à la vitre de son petit pied chaussé de bleu et danse, danse de joie, de froid pour réchauffer son cœur, son cœur de bois porte-bonheur. La nuit, elle lève ses bras suppliants vers les étoiles.

LE VENT ET L'ESPRIT

C'est une étonnante chimère. La tête, plus haut que cet étage, se place entre les deux fils de fer et se cale et se tient; rien ne bouge.

La tête inconnue parle et je ne comprends aucun mot, je n'entends aucun son — bas contre terre. Je suis toujours sur le trottoir d'en face et je regarde; je regarde les mots qu'emporte le vent; les mots qu'il va jeter plus loin. La tête parle et je n'entends rien, le vent disperse tout.

O grand vent, moqueur ou lugubre, j'ai souhaité ta mort. Et je perds mon chapeau que tu m'as pris aussi. Je n'ai plus rien; mais ma haine dure, hélas plus que toi-même.

FETISH

Tiny doll and marionette for a charm, thrashing about at my window by the will of the wind. Rain has dampened her dress, her face, and her hands whose color is fading. She has even lost a leg. But her ring remains and with it, her power. In wintertime, she raps against the windowpane with her little blue-shod foot and dances, dances for joy. With cold to warm up her heart, her charmed-wood heart. Nightly, she lifts her arms in supplication toward the stars.

THE WIND AND THE SPIRIT

An astonishing chimera. The head, higher than this room, fits between the two wires, settles, and is still: nothing moves.

The unknown head speaks and I grasp not a word, hear not a sound — low as the earth. I am still on the sidewalk opposite and I am looking, looking at the words the wind carries off, the words it will later cast away. The head speaks and I hear nothing, the wind disperses everything.

Oh great wind, mocking or lugubrious. I have longed for your death. Deprived of my hat you've snatched from me too. I have nothing any longer; but my hatred endures, alas, longer than you.

HIVER

À travers la pluie dense et glacée de ce soir-là où le boulevard s'éclaire, un petit homme noir au visage bleui. Est-ce de froid? Est-ce du feu interne qu'allume l'alcool?

Mais ses souliers trop grands sont pleins d'eau et il tourne autour des réverbères. C'est la joie et la pitié des filles. Quelle lourde émotion! Qui voudra l'enlever.

O monde sans abri qui vas ce dur chemin et qui t'en moques, je ne te comprends pas. J'aime la tiédeur, le confort et la quiétude.

O monde qui les méprises, tu me fais peur!

HOTELS

Dans une singulière détresse d'or j'attends, passé minuit, que vienne l'heure propice à toutes les défenses contre les éléments. Je vais passer devant l'ennemi, redoutable plus que la pluie, plus que le froid. Il dort et ma main tremble. Une petite arme me suffira, mais avec ce terrible bruit dans la serrure et de la porte, je vais être assailli d'horribles cauchemars.

Au matin nouveau, départ à pas de chat. C'est un autre soupir et la rue me devient moins hostile; mais quand viendront, enfin, la délivrance et le repos tranquille? Cependant je me souviens d'avoir dormi dans un lit plus doux dressé pour moi.

Il n'en reste plus que les rêves.

WINTER

Through the dense and icy rain of that evening when the boulevard lights up, a small black man with a face gone blue. From the cold? Or the internal blaze drink has kindled?

But his shoes, too large for him, are water-clogged, and he circles around the street lamps. He's the joy and the pity of the whores. What a weight of feeling! Who'd agree to remove it?

Oh shelterless world along this harsh path, uncaring, I don't understand you. I like things tepid, comfortable, and tranquil.

Oh world disdaining these things, you frighten me.

HOTELS

In an odd golden distress I have been waiting, past midnight, for the time propitious for all possible defenses against the elements. I shall pass before the enemy, more to be feared than rain, more than cold. He sleeps and my hand trembles. A small weapon will suffice, but with this terrible noise in the keyhole and at the door, I shall be prey to horrendous nightmares.

In the fresh morning, departure quiet as a cat. Another sigh and the street becomes less hostile for me; but when will I have deliverance and peaceful rest? However I remember having slept in a softer bed made up for me.

Of it only dreams remain.

CARNAVAL

Les tapis fortement secoués laissaient des signes entre les arbres. On les avait déteints avec les pieds.

Sur les quais, avec un regard attendri, les têtes se tournaient, mais les passants gardaient leur masque.

Toute la perspective se bariolait en tapis déteints ou plus riches et parfois on entendait des cris qui proclamaient la honte de ceux qu'on attaquait. Le soir la lumière et les ombres se battent. Masquée, toute la haine se choque et le mieux caché devient le plus hardi.

C'est un grand divertissement général, un jeu et ce jeu c'est encore une lutte.

LES POÈTES

Sa tête s'abritait craintivement sous l'abat-jour de la lampe. Il est vert et ses yeux sont rouges. Il y a un musicien qui ne bouge pas. Il dort; ses mains coupées jouent du violon pour lui faire oublier sa misère.

Un escalier qui ne conduit nulle part grimpe autour de la maison. Il n'y a, d'ailleurs, ni portes ni fenêtres. On voit sur le toit s'agiter des ombres qui se précipitent dans le vide. Elles tombent une à une et ne se tuent pas. Vite par l'escalier elles remontent et recommencent, éternellement charmées par le musicien qui joue toujours du violon avec ses mains qui ne l'écoutent pas.

CARNIVAL

The rugs briskly shaken out left signs between the trees. Feet had discolored them.

On the wharfs, the heads turned, tenderness in their gaze, but the passersby kept their masks.

The whole perspective turned multi-striped in rugs discolored or richer, and sometimes cries announced the shame of those attacked. In the evening, light and the shadows struggle. Masked, the totality of hatred collides and the most cleverly hidden becomes the most daring.

A great general diversion, a game and this game is still a struggle.

THE POETS

His head took shelter fearfully under the lamp shade. He is green, his eyes red. There is a musician who does not move. He sleeps: his severed hands play the violin to help him forget his misery.

A staircase leading nowhere climbs round the house. Nor are there any doors or windows. On the roof shadows can be seen shifting about and hurtling into emptiness. One by one they fall, unharmed. Quickly they move back up the stairs and start again, eternally charmed by the violinist still playing, his hands not listening.

TRAITS ET FIGURES

Une éclaircie avec du bleu dans le ciel; dans la forêt des clairières toutes vertes; mais dans la ville où le dessin nous emprisonne, l'arc de cercle du porche, les carrés des fenêtres, les losanges des toits.

Des lignes, rien que des lignes, pour la commodité des bâtisses humaines.

Dans ma tête des lignes, rien que des lignes; si je pouvais y mettre un peu d'ordre seulement.

A L'AUBE

Dans mon rêve la tête d'un enfant était au centre.

Si les nuages s'accumulent sur ton toit et que la pluie t'épargne garderas-tu le secret de ce double miracle?

Mais aucune voix ne t'appelle. Si tu te lèves, pieds nus, tu prendras mal. Où irais-tu d'ailleurs, à travers ces ravins de lumières.

L'édredon gardait le silence; les jambes repliées sous lui il marche sur ses ailes et sort. C'était un ange et le matin plus blanc qui se levait.

STROKES AND FIGURES

A blue-tinged clearing in the sky; in the forest, clearings quite green; but in the town where pattern imprisons us, the arch of the porch circle, the squares of windows, the diamonds of the roofs.

Lines, nothing but lines, for the convenience of human buildings.

In my head lines, nothing but lines; if only I could make some order of them.

AT DAWN

In my dream a child's bed was at the center.

If the clouds accumulate on your roof and the rain spares you, will you keep the secret of this double miracle?

But no voice calls you. If you rise barefooted, you will catch a cold. Where would you go anyway, across these ravines of lights?

The eiderdown kept still. His legs folded under him, he walks on his wings and departs, an angel and the whiter morn arising.

INCOGNITO

Une première fois sa canne tombe et il remonte sur le trottoir.

La jambe droite s'écarte de la ligne du triangle et, de dos, son âge l'accompagne. Serait-il si vieux?

Son temps se passe à déjouer la stratégie des filles. Au carrefour il s'évanouit dans l'ombre et la voiture l'emporte.

C'était peut-être un roi, déguisé en vieillard timide et malheureux.

LE VOYAGEUR ET SON OMBRE

Il faisait si chaud qu'il laissait au courant de la route tous ses vêtements un à un. Il les laissait accrochés aux buissons. Et, quand il fut nu, il s'approchait déjà de la ville. Une honte immense s'empara de lui et l'empêcha d'entrer. Il était nu et comment ne pas attirer les regards?

Alors il contourna la ville et entra par la porte opposée. Il avait pris la place de son ombre qui, passant la première, le protégeait.

INCOGNITO

For the first time his cane falls and he climbs back up on the sidewalk.

The right leg leaves the triangle's line, and from behind, his age moves along with him. Could he be so old?

His time is spent foiling the strategy of the girls. At the crossroads he faints in the shadow and the coach bears him away.

Perhaps he was a king, disguised as an old man, timid and unhappy.

THE TRAVELER AND HIS SHADOW

It was so hot that he shed his clothes one by one along the road. He left them hanging on the shrubs. And when he was naked, he was already nearing the town. An immense shame came over him and kept him from entering. He was naked, and how could he help being stared at?

Then he went round the town and entered by the opposite gate. He had taken the place of his shadow which, going first, protected him.

L'AIR MEURTRI

Il fait si chaud que l'air vibre et que tout bruit devient assourdissant. Des meutes de chiens féroces aboient. Par les fenêtres ouvertes, les cris des femmes rivalisent avec cette fanfare barbare.

Le froid a de la peine à geler ces paroles. Si les oiseaux se taisaient, si les femmes se taisaient, si les chiens étaient morts . . . Un moment les jardins sont calmes et tout s'endort; mais bientôt le terrible bruit recommence. Ce sont les appels du soleil et chacun y répond avec exubérance. Quelques êtres muets qu'on accable ne peuvent protester ni se venger. Le bruit souverain les opprime.

Dans les fumées, par-dessus les toits qui s'en préservent seuls, j'aurais fait tournoyer ma tête comme un grelot sans pois au bout d'une ficelle. La vitesse ouatée jusqu'aux nuages et permettre au ruisseau de murmurer tout seul!

Le ciel est descendu, on a refermé les fenêtres et les bouches sont closes. Après la chute des feuilles les oiseaux même n'osent plus gazouiller. Il fait si froid.

L'hiver c'est l'intervalle du silence.

THE BRUISED AIR

It is so hot that the air vibrates and any noise deafens. Hordes of ferocious dogs are barking. Through the open windows, the cries of the women vie with this barbaric fanfare.

The cold can scarcely freeze these words. If birds kept silent, if women hushed, if dogs were dead . . . For a moment, the gardens are calm and all drifts back to sleep; but soon the fearful noise begins once more . . . These are the summons of the sun and everyone answers with exuberance. Some mute and burdened beings can neither protest nor avenge themselves. The noise in its dominance oppresses them.

In the smoke above the roofs which alone stay out of the din, I would have had my head spin about like the clapper of the empty sleighbell. Muffled speed up to the clouds and let the stream murmur all alone!

The heavens descended, the windows have been closed again, and the mouths also. After the fall of leaves even the birds dare not chirp. It is so cold.

Winter is the interval of silence.

LA REPASSEUSE

Autrefois ses mains faisaient des taches roses sur le linge éclatant qu'elle repassait. Mais dans la boutique où le poêle est trop rouge son sang s'est peu à peu évaporé. Elle devient de plus en plus blanche et dans la vapeur qui monte on la distingue à peine au milieu des vagues luisantes des dentelles.

Ses cheveux blonds flottent dans l'air en boucles de rayons et le fer continue sa route en soulevant du linge des nuages — et autour de la table son âme qui résiste encore, son âme de repasseuse court et plie comme le linge en fredonnant une chanson — sans que personne y prenne garde.

UNE APPARENCE MÉDIOCRE

Le train siffle et repart dans la fumée qui se fond au ciel bas.

C'est un long convoi de larmes et sur chaque quai où l'on se sépare de nouveaux bras agitent des mouchoirs. Mais celui-là est seul et ses lunettes se ternissent des larmes des autres ou de la pluie qui fouette la vitre où il colle son nez. Il n'a quitté personne et nul ne l'attendra à la gare où il va descendre.

D'ailleurs il ne raconte pas ses voyages, il ne sait pas décrire les pays qu'il a vus. Il n'a rien vu peut-être, et quand on le regarde, de peur qu'on l'interroge, il baisse les yeux ou les lève vers le ciel où d'autres nuages se fondent. À l'arrivée, sans expression de joie ou d'impatience, il part, seul dans la nuit, et, sous les becs de gaz qui l'éclairent par intervalles, on le voit disparaître, sa petite valise à la main. Il est seul, on le croit seul. Pourtant quelque chose le suit ou peut-être quelqu'un dans la forme étrange de son ombre.

THE GIRL IRONING

Once her hands used to make rose colored spots on the gleaming linen she ironed. But in the shop where the stove is too hot her blood has evaporated little by little. She becomes whiter and whiter and in the rising steam you can barely make her out among the lace in its shiny undulations.

Her blonde hair floats in the air in radiant curls and the iron continues its path, raising clouds from the linen — and around the table her soul still resisting, her ironing girl's soul runs about and is pleated like the linen humming a song — without anyone noticing.

A MEDIOCRE APPEARANCE

The train whistles and sets off again in the smoke melting in the low sky.

Tears in a long convoy and on each track where people part, other arms wave handkerchiefs. But that one is alone and his glasses mist with others' tears or with the rain lashing the windowpane where his nose presses. He has left no one and will be met by no one at the station.

Nor does he tell about his trips, unable to describe the countries he has seen. Perhaps he has seen nothing and when he is looked at, fearful lest he be asked a question, he lowers his eyes or raises them toward the sky where other clouds are melting. At his arrival, with no expression of joy or impatience, he sets off alone in the night, and under the gas lamps lighting him now and again, he is seen disappearing, his small suitcase in his hand. He is alone, seems to be alone. Still, something is following him or perhaps someone in the strange form of his shadow.

L'INTRUS

Entre les 4 murs de cette salle basse se mouvaient des esprits obscurs et d'autres extrêmement légers et lumineux.

Un homme presque nu entra au milieu de ces toiles et dans ces étendues de glace et de désert.

Il entraînait une caravane en désordre et marchait seul. Une voix qui venait d'ailleurs faisait tinter à nos oreilles un son nouveau. Mais dans ce mélange de capes et d'épées, de chansons et de cris, il régnait un air de carnaval — il y manquait surtout la grâce avec l'esprit.

Un monde très ancien tournoyait dans nos têtes et l'on attendait le moment où tout allait tomber.

Mais, dehors, au lieu d'un clair de lune sur un fond de décor — on trouvait un temps gris où manœuvraient les machines hurlantes dissipant le malaise. Dans la rue, nous avions retrouvé la foule et notre siècle. Mais tous ces esprits obscurs ou lumineux, légers et lourds, et l'homme nu de quelle époque étaient-ils descendus ce soir-là?

THE INTRUDER

Between the 4 walls of this low room, somber spirits wandered, and others extremely light and luminous.

A man almost naked entered amid these canvasses and in these stretches of ice and desert.

With him he brought a caravan of disorder and walked alone. A voice which came from elsewhere rang a new sound in our ears. But in this mixture of capes and swords, of songs and shouts, a carnival air reigned — above all grace was missing, and wit.

An ancient world spun about in our heads and we awaited the moment when everything would collapse.

But outside, instead of moonlight on a theatre backdrop, there was a gray weather, where shrieking machines were to dissipate anxiety. In the street we had found the crowd once more and our own century. But from what epoch had there come all these somber or luminous spirits, light and heavy, and the naked man that evening?

BELLE ÉTOILE

J'aurai peut-être perdu la clé, et tout le monde rit autour de moi et chacun me montre une clé énorme pendue à son cou.

Je suis le seul à ne rien avoir pour entrer quelque part. Ils ont tous disparu et les portes closes laissent la rue plus triste. Personne. Je frapperai partout.

Des injures jaillissent des fenêtres et je m'éloigne.

Alors un peu plus loin que la ville, au bord d'une rivière et d'un bois, j'ai trouvé une porte. Une simple porte à claire-voie et sans serrure. Je me suis mis derrière et, sous la nuit qui n'a pas de fenêtres mais de larges rideaux, entre la forêt et la rivière qui me protègent, j'ai pu dormir.

CIVIL

Après cette scène où je me suis montré si éclatant de chasteté que peut-il advenir?

Où sont mes papiers et mon identité vieillie et la date de ma naissance imprécise? Et, d'ailleurs, suis-je encore celui de la dernière fois? Pourtant je croyais avoir repris suffisamment de forces. Et tout ce qu'on m'avait promis.

La tête s'écarte de la ligne bleue qui se déroule sur la longue route rugueuse. En dehors d'elle aucun salut possible et l'indifférence nous perd.

Voilà pour ta modestie, ton abstinence et ta faiblesse, sans cruauté. Mille dangers à craindre. Regarde, tourne ton œil vers cette nappe noire.

Sur le trottoir le gendarme souverain t'arrête d'un appel bref de sa question brutale.

UNDER THE STARS

I have in all likelihood lost the key and everyone laughs all about me, each one showing me a mammoth key hung about his neck.

I am the only one with no place to enter. They have all disappeared and the closed doors leave the street sadder. No one. I shall knock everywhere.

Insults lash forth from windows and I go on.

Then a way past the town, at the edge of a river and a wood, I found a door. A simple wicket gate and no lock. I placed myself behind it and, under the night with no windows but wide curtains, between the forest and the river protecting me, I could sleep.

CIVIL

After this scene where I revealed myself so resplendently chaste what can happen?

Where are my papers and my identity grown old and the date of my imprecise birth? And besides, am I still the one from last time? Yet I thought I had gotten strong enough again. And everything I'd been promised.

The head moves away from the blue line unrolling down the long uneven road. Apart from it no salvation is possible and indifference destroys us.

So much for your modesty, your abstinence and your weakness, devoid of cruelty. A thousand dangers to fear. Look, gaze upon this black surface.

On the sidewalk the domineering gendarme stops you with a terse summons for a brutal questioning.

CORTÈGE

Quand les premiers furent passés et que l'on attendait encore.

Une voix s'éleva qui t'avertit.

Quand les derniers furent passés et que l'on n'entendit plus rien.

Qui t'a dit de rester là encore?

La dernière étoile résistait au matin et tu ne pouvais plus voir que la poussière. Sous tes pieds il n'y avait plus que de la poussière au loin et partout, et aussi tes souliers en étaient recouverts.

Et ce soir-là les questions t'accablèrent.

Tu les as vus passer et tu restes là. Le chant du coq t'avertit, le chant du coq ou la poussière t'avertissent que tes paupières sont lourdes, tes cils sont gris comme les buissons au bord de la route; il est temps d'aller dormir. Et tu les reverras peut-être tous en rêve.

PROCESSION

When the first ones had gone by and people were still waiting.

A voice was raised to warn you.

When the last ones had gone by and nothing more was heard.

Who told you to stay on there?

The last star was resisting the morning and you could no longer see anything but dust. Under your feet there was no longer anything but dust far off and everywhere: your shoes too were covered with it.

And that evening the questions assaulted you.

You saw them go by and you remain there. The cock's cry warns you, the cock's cry or the dust warn you that your eyelids are heavy, your lashes grey like the shrubs along the road; it is time to go and sleep. And perhaps you will see them all again, dreaming.

TIMIDITÉ

Après un voyage trop long et des insomnies prolongée, seule la plus grande joie vient t'attendre.

Sans aucune certitude ni garantie avec tous les efforts, seulement permis et promis, tu n'es plus seul et prêt à marcher, n'importe où.

Le monde te confie sa force en échange de ta confiance. Tu ferais toutes les démarches si l'aplomb avait payé ton sort à ta naissance. Mais qui t'a mis cette hésitation poignante dans le ventre? Tes jambes n'auront jamais la force de ton énorme poids.

Sur le palier, plus haut que les marches qu'il n'a pas su compter, il hésite et, plus heureux qu'après une grande victoire, il redescend sans avoir seulement effleuré de sa main lâche le cordon auquel il aurait plutôt pendu son cou.

TIMIDITY

After too long a trip and prolonged insomnia, only the greatest joy comes to await you.

With no certainty or guarantee from all the effort, only permitted and promised, you are no longer alone and ready to walk no matter where.

The world entrusts you with its strength in exchange for your confidence. You would make all the moves if aplomb had paid for your fate at birth. But who put this poignant hesitation in·you? Your legs will never have the strength of your enormous weight.

On the landing, higher than the steps he never managed to count, he hesitates, and happier than after a great victory, he comes back down without having even so much as grazed with his limp hand the cord on which he would sooner have hung his neck.

APRÈS LE BAL

J'ai peut-être mis au vestiaire plus que mes vêtements. Je m'avance, allégé, avec trop d'assurance et quelqu'un dans la salle a remarqué mes pas. Les rayons sont pleins de danseuses.

Je tourne, je tourne sans rien voir dans les flots de rayons des lampes électriques et je marche sur tant de pieds et tant d'autres meurtrissent les miens.

Quel bal, quelle fête! J'ai trouvé toutes les femmes belles, tous mes désirs volent vers tous ces yeux. Tant qu'a duré l'orchestre j'ai tourné des talons sur un parquet ciré, plein d'émotion, et mes bras sont rompus d'avoir supporté tant de proies qu'il a fallu lâcher.

Mais l'orchestre s'est tu, les lampes éteintes ont laissé s'alourdir la fatigue. Au vestiaire, on m'a rendu un chaud manteau contre le gel, mais le reste? Il me manque pourtant quelque chose. Je suis seul et je ne puis lutter contre ce froid.

AFTER THE BALL

Perhaps I have left more than just my clothes in the cloakroom. I move forward, lightened, with too much self-assurance, and someone in the room has noticed my step. The light beams are filled with dancing women.

I am spinning, spinning about and seeing nothing in the beams flooding from the electric lights and walking on so many feet and so many others bruise mine.

What a dance, what a ball: I found the women lovely, and my desires rush forward toward those eyes. As long as the orchestra lasted, I spun my heels about on a waxed floor, full of emotion, and my arms are exhausted from propping up the preys I had then to desert.

But the orchestra fell silent, the extinguished lamps let my fatigue grow heavy. In the cloakroom they gave me back a warm coat against the frost, but the rest? Something still is missing. Alone, I cannot struggle against this cold.

VOYAGES TROP GRANDS

C'était peut-être la première fois qu'il voyait quelque chose de clair. Il se sentait accroché au dernier wagon du train de luxe pour quelque destination magnifique et regardait distraitement le paysage qui allait, à rebours, bien plus vite que lui. Avec la somme de tous les détails perdus on aurait fait un nouveau monde; mais lui n'avait besoin de rien. De son rôle, qu'il jouait avec le plus grand sérieux, il lui manquait la signification.

Les plus grandes gares n'avaient pas assez de bruit pour l'émouvoir; au coin de toutes les collines il comprenait mieux l'isolement des maisons blanches. Quand on longeait la mer il ne voyait que les voiles des barques qui en précisaient l'étendue.

Tout est inerte et trop grand pour ses yeux et son cœur. Sa tête doit rester vide et rien ne pourrait la remplir.

Quand il revenait enfin là d'où il était parti, sa tâche bien remplie, sa journée faite il ne pensait qu'au petit coin de terre où sa vie contenait, où il aurait la place juste pour mourir.

CHACUN SA PART

Il a chassé la lune, il a laissé la nuit. Une à une les étoiles sont tombées dans un filet d'eau vive.

Derrière les trembles un étrange pêcheur guette avec impatience d'un œil ouvert, le seul, caché sous son large chapeau; et la ligne frémit.

Rien ne se prend, mais il emplit sa gibecière de pièces d'or dont l'éclat s'est éteint dans le panier fermé.

Mais un autre attendait plus loin du bord. Plus modeste il pêchait dans la flaque de boue qu'avait laissée la pluie. Cette eau, venue du ciel, était pleine d'étoiles.

TRIPS IN EXCESS

It was perhaps the first time he had seen anything clear. He felt hooked to the last car of the first-class train headed for some magnificent destination and looked absent-mindedly at the land-scape, which was going backwards much faster than he was. A new world could have been created with all the lost details; but he needed nothing. He saw no meaning in his role, which he was playing with the greatest possible seriousness.

The greatest stations did not have enough noise to move him; in the corner of all the hills he better understood the isolation of the white houses. When they went alongside the sea, he saw only the sails of the boats, revealing its reach.

Everything is inert and too large for his eyes and his heart. His head had to remain empty and nothing could ever fill it.

When he came back at last to the place where he had started, his task completed, his day finished, he thought only of the little corner of earth where his life fit in, where he would have just enough room to die.

TO EACH HIS SHARE

He chased the moon and left the night. One by one the stars fell into a net of living water.

Behind the quaking aspens, a strange fisherman waits impa-tiently, with one eye open, the only one, hidden under his wide hat; and the line quivers.

Nothing gets caught, but he fills his game-bag with gold pieces whose gleam is extinguished in the closed basket.

But another is waiting further from the shore. More mod-estly, he was fishing in the mud puddle left by the rain. This water, having come from the sky, was filled with stars.

BRUITS DE NUIT

Au moment où les chevaux passaient, la suspension trembla. Le plafond menaçait de se pencher à droite, contre nos têtes; mais les fenêtres restaient d'aplomb avec le ciel, et l'on voyait le paysage nocturne.

Il n'y avait plus de hiboux dans les ruines, plus de rayon de lune parmi les arbres, mais une cheminée d'usine et — autour — des maisons dont les toits avaient l'air de grandir.

Et les chevaux — dont on entendait les pas précipités — transportaient dans la nuit complice des fourgons de mort en métal.

FRONTS DE BATAILLE

Sur le rempart où tremblent des ruines on entend un écho de tambours. On les avait crevés. Ceux d'hier se répondent encore.

La nuit finie, le bruit dissipe les rêves et les fronts découverts où saigne une blessure.

Au milieu des fumées les hommes sont perdus et déjà le soleil transperce l'horizon.

Qui sonna la victoire? La charge bat pour ceux qui sont tombés!

Une trompette rallie des lambeaux d'escadrons et la fumée soutient les chevaux dont les pieds ne touchent plus le sol.

Mais celui qui les aurait peints n'était plus là.

NIGHT SOUNDS

At the moment when the horses were passing by the hanging lamp started to quiver. The ceiling threatened to lean to the right, against our heads; but the windows remained upright with the sky, and the nocturnal landscape was visible.

No longer were there owls among the ruins, nor moon beams among the trees, but a factory chimney and — around it — houses whose roofs seemed to grow.

And the horses — whose hurried steps were heard — transported into the accomplice night the metal wagons of death.

BATTLEFRONTS

On the rampart where ruins are trembling an echo of drums is heard. They had been shattered. Those of yesterday still respond to each other now.

Once night is finished, the noise dissipates the dreams and the bared foreheads where a wound is bleeding.

Amid the smoke, men are lost and already the sun pierces through the horizon.

Who rang the sounds of victory: The volley laments those fallen.

A trumpet rallies the tatters of squadrons and the smoke holds up the horses whose hoofs no longer touch the ground.

But he who would have painted them was no longer there.

BATAILLE

Dans la poitrine, l'amour d'un drapeau décoloré par les pluies. Dans ma tête, les tambours battent. Mais d'où vient l'ennemi?

Si ta foi est morte que répondre à leur commandement?

Un ami meurt d'enthousiasme derrière ses canons et sa fatigue est plus forte que tout.

Et, dans les champs bordés de routes, au coin des bois qui ont une autre forme parce qu'il y a des hommes cachés, il se promène, macabre comme la mort, malgré son ventre.

Les ruines balancent leurs cadavres et des têtes sans képis.

Ce tableau, soldat, quand le finiras-tu? Ai-je rêvé que j'y étais encore? Je faisais, en tout cas, un drôle de métier.

Quand le soleil, que j'avais pris pour un éclair, darda son rayon sur mon oreille sourde, je me désaltérais, sous les saules vert et blanc, dans un ruisseau d'eau rose.

J'avais si soif!

FACE A FACE

Il s'avance et la raideur de son pas timide trahit son assurance. Les regards ne quittent pas ses pieds. Tout ce qui luit dans ces yeux, d'où jaillissent de mauvaises pensées, éclaire sa marche hésitante. Il va tomber.

Au fond de la salle une image connue se dresse. Sa main tendue va vers la sienne. Il ne voit plus rien que ça; mais il se heurte, tout à coup, contre lui-même.

BATTLE

In the chest the love of a flag discolored by the rains. In my head drums are beating. But where is the enemy coming from?

If your faith is dead, what will you answer to their command?

A friend dies from enthusiasm behind his cannons and his fatigue is stronger than all else.

And in the fields bordered by the roads, in the corner of the woods differently-shaped because of the men hidden there, he walks, macabre as death, in spite of his stomach.

The ruins dangle their cadavers and hatless heads.

This painting, soldier, when will you finish it? Did I dream I was still there? In any case I was doing a funny job.

When the sun, which I'd taken for a lightning flash, darted its beam on my deaf ear, I quenched my thirst, under the green and white willows, in a stream of pink water.

I was so thirsty!

FACE TO FACE

He is moving forward and the stiffness of his timid step belies his assurance. Attention is focused on his feet. Everything shining in these eyes, which radiate evil thoughts, makes clear the hesitation of his gait. He is about to fall.

In the back of the room a well-known figure stands up. Its hand, held out, reaches for his. He sees only that and nothing else; but he collides, suddenly, with himself.

SALTIMBANQUES

Au milieu de cet attroupement il y a avec un enfant qui danse un homme qui soulève des poids. Ses bras tatoués de bleu prennent le ciel à témoin de leur force inutile.

L'enfant danse, léger, dans un maillot trop grand; plus léger que les boules où il se tient en équilibre. Et quand il tend son escarcelle, personne ne donne. Personne ne donne de peur de la remplir d'un poids trop lourd. Il est si maigre.

CRÉPUSCULE

Le soir tombant dilatait les yeux du chat.

Nous étions tous les deux assis sur la fenêtre et nous regardions, nous écoutions tout ce qui n'était pas autre part qu'en nous-mêmes.

Derrière la ligne qui fermait la rue, la ligne d'en haut, les arbres découpaient de la dentelle sur le ciel.

Et la ville, où est-elle la ville qui se noie au fond dans l'eau qui forme les nuages?

ACROBATS

In the middle of the crowd there is, with a dancing child, a man lifting weights. His arms tattooed in blue call on the sky to bear witness to their useless strength.

Lightly, the child dances, in tights which are too big for him; lighter than the balls he balances on. And when he holds out his purse, no one gives anything. No one gives for fear of making it too heavy. He is so thin.

TWILIGHT

The fall of evening dilated the cat's eyes.

We were both seated by the window and looking, listening to everything which was nowhere but in ourselves.

Behind the line closing the street, and above it, the trees traced patterns of lace cut-outs upon the sky.

And the town, where is the town submerged in the depths of the water forming the clouds?

L'ENVERS A L'ENDROIT

Il grimpe sans jamais s'arrêter, sans jamais se retourner et personne que lui ne sait où il va.

Le poids qu'il traîne est lourd mais ses jambes sont libres et il n'a pas d'oreilles.

A chaque porte il a crié son nom, personne n'a ouvert.

Mais quand il a su qu'on attendait quelqu'un et qui, il a su transformer son visage. Alors il est entré à la place de celui qu'on attendait et qui ne venait pas.

LES PENSÉES BASSES

Les quatre pieds de la table sont immobiles; les autres aussi. Et vos têtes! Vos têtes qui se penchent dans vos mains pour ne pas qu'on les voie rougir?

THE WRONG SIDE ON THE RIGHT SIDE

He climbs, never stopping, never turning around, and no one but himself knows where he is going.

The weight he drags along is heavy, but his legs are free and he has no ears.

At each door he shouted his name; no one opened.

But when he found out they were awaiting someone and whom, he was able to alter his face. Then he entered in the place of the one awaited, who never came.

LOW THOUGHTS

The four feet of the table are immobile; the others too. And your faces! Your faces cupped in your hands so no one will see them blushing?

CARRÉS

Le masque honteux cachait ses dents. Un autre œil voyait qu'elles étaient fausses. Où cela se passe-t-il? Et quand? Il est seul, il pleure, malgré l'orgueil qui le soutient, et il devient laid. Parce qu'il a plu sur les souliers, disait l'autre, de la salive sur mes souliers, je suis devenu pâle et méchant. Et il embrassa le masque qui le mordit en ricanant.

Le profil, le même profil que la grande chanteuse! Elle voulait l'avoir, elle l'eut et aussi son immense bouche sans sa voix. Mais ce qu'elle enviait le plus c'était sa robe et jamais elle ne put l'avoir.

Si vous entendez der-
rière vous faire Psst et
qu'en même temps passe
un taxi ne vous retour-
nez pas . . . c'est pour le
taxi.

Les cheveux coupés, la
tête tranchée, le sabre
restait encore entre ses
dents. Le bourreau
amateur pleurait et sa
figure était un masque.
On l'avait importé de
Chine et il ne savait
plus être cruel.

Je passe en m'engouf-
frant, je m'engouffre
en passant. Quel gouf-
fre! La tête qui tour-
nait autour de moi
a disparu. — Les
Oiseaux chantaient
derrière la fenêtre; ils
chantaient faux et
n'étaient pas en plumes
véritables.

Le rhum est excellent
la pipe est amère et les
étoiles qui tombent de
vos cheveux s'envolent
dans la cheminée.

De la reliure de tes
lèvres de la reliure de
tes volets de la reliure
de nos mains. O peut-
être plus facile. Sur le
balcon de bois elle
montait la garde en
chemise éclatante.

Après les premiers pas
sur les pointes il avait
pris son vol. Les pre-
miers nuages l'arrê-
tent. Ce sont des
glaces. Et là, où il re-
trouvait notre monde
sans la chair, il se crut
au ciel.

SQUARES

The shameful mask hid his teeth.
Another eye saw they were false. Where
is it happening? And when? He is alone,
weeping, despite the pride bearing him
up, and he becomes ugly. Because it has
rained on the shoes, the other one said,
saliva on my shoes, I have become pale
and wicked. And he kissed the mask
which bit him as it sneered.

The profile, the same
profile as the great singer!
She wanted to have it, she
had it and also her
mammoth mouth without
her voice. But what she
most envied was her dress
and never could she have it.

If you hear someone be-
hind you go Psst and a
taxi is passing at the
same time don't turn
around . . . it's for the
taxi.

The hair cut, the head sev-
ered, the saber still remained
between his teeth. The am-
ateur executioner was weep-
ing and his face was a mask.
He had been imported from
China and no longer knew
how to be cruel.

I pass by being swallowed
up, am swallowed up in a
passing by. What an abyss!
The head turning about me
has disappeared. The birds
were singing behind the win-
dow; they were singing off-
key and were not dressed in
real feathers.

The rum is excellent
The pipe is bitter and
the stars falling from
your hair take off in
the fireplace.

From the binding of your lips
from the binding of your
shutters from the binding of
our hands. Or perhaps easier.
On the wooden balcony she
kept watch in a dazzling
nightgown.

After the first steps on his
toes he had taken flight. The
first clouds stop him. They
are mirrors. And here again,
where he discovered our world
without flesh, he believed
himself in heaven.

TOUJOURS GÊNÉ

Qui m'a révélé l'endroit précis. Le ciel où les deux murs se joignent. L'angle où l'on est à l'abri?

Par-dessus, le vent emporte la terre qui se déplace. Quelques nids sont tombés et l'on entend des cris qui viennent des fenêtres. C'est là qu'on attend. C'est de là qu'on regarde et qu'on nous surprend. L'affreuse tête qui se balance sur le toit en ricanant!
Ni le mur ni les arbres ne sont assez grands.

Et déjà vous commencez à rougir plus que moi-même. Allons-nous-en.

AUTRE FACE

Les yeux noirs! Mais ce sont des lorgnons! Une ombre glisse sur les joues. Deux larmes qui coulent sur les joues. Est-ce pour moi ou bien à cause du soleil? Personne n'ose demander qui ils regardent et chacun prend ce regard pour soi. Je crains d'être trop petit et trop loin. Moi, je suis certainement trop loin et celui qui est devant moi se rapproche. Pour me rassurer je me dis que les yeux ne peuvent pas tout voir et qu'il ne reste au cœur rien que ce qu'il peut contenir.

ALWAYS BOTHERED

Who revealed to me the precise place. They sky where the two walls join. The angle where you are sheltered?

Above, the wind carries off the earth which shifts position. A few nests have fallen and you hear cries coming from the windows. The waiting place, where they look out, and catch us off guard. The awful head as it sways sneering on the roof.

Neither the wall nor the trees are tall enough.

And you are already beginning to blush more than I am. Let's go away.

ANOTHER FACE

Two black eyes! But those are opera glasses! A shadow slides over the cheeks. Two tears are running down the cheeks. Because of me or then because of the sun? No one dares to ask who they are looking at and each one takes this look for himself. I fear I am too little and too far off. I am certainly too far off and the one before me comes nearer. For reassurance, I tell myself that eyes cannot see everything and that there remains in the heart nothing but what it can contain.

SON SEUL PASSAGE

Sur le bord du chemin où il s'est laissé tomber, les bras pendants, ses mains traînent dans le ruisseau où l'eau ne coule pas. La forêt s'ouvre sur sa tête et d'en haut le passant regarde le chemin. Il attend; aucun bruit ne court ailleurs que dans les branches où passe le vent. Le silence a désolé son cœur solitaire et fermé.

Un chien qui mord, une roue qui crie sur le gravier un moment secoueraient sa torpeur. Mais pour lui le monde est une route interminable où l'on se perd. Il a laissé dans les buissons ses souvenirs et les années passées sans rien comprendre.

La forêt qui l'arrête est un abri où il fuit le soleil et il regarde, sans la voir, monter la route vers les arbres. Plus loin le village s'endort étendu dans les champs que la nuit assombrit, mais pas une fenêtre en l'éclairant ne lui sourit.

HIS ONLY PASSAGE

At pathside where he let himself fall, his arms dragging, his hands are trailing in the stream where the water does not run. The forest opens over his head and from above, the passerby contemplates the path. He is waiting; no sound but in the branches where the wind is moving. The silence has made desolation in his closed and solitary heart.

A dog biting, a wheel screeching on the gravel for an instant would shake off his torpor. But for him the world is an interminable road where one is lost. In the bushes he has left his memories and the years which have passed by with no understanding.

The forest which stops him is a shelter for him to flee the sun, and he looks at the road climbing towards the trees, not seeing it. Further on, the village dozes stretched out in the fields made somber by the night, but not a window lighting up for him.

LES CORPS RIDICULES DES ESPRITS

Un cortège de gens plus ou moins honorables. Quelques-uns sourient dans le vide avec sérénité. Ils sont nus. Une auréole à la tête des premiers qui ont su prendre la place. Les plus petits en queue.

On passe entre les arbres qui s'inclinent. Les esprits qui se sont réfugiés derrière les étoiles regardent. La curiosité vient de partout. La route s'illumine.

Dans le silence digne, si quelqu'un chante c'est une douce voix qui monte et personne ne rit. La chanson est connue de tous.

On passe devant la maison d'un poète qui n'est pas là. La pluie qui tombait sur son piano, à travers le toit, l'a chassé.

Bientôt, c'est un boulevard bordé de cafés où la foule s'ennuie. Tout le monde se lève. Le cortège a grossi.

Enfin par l'avenue qui monte la file des gens s'éloigne, les derniers paraissent les plus grands. Les premiers ont déjà disparu.

Derrière un monument d'une époque oubliée le soleil se lève en rayons séparés et l'ombre des passants lentement s'efface. Les rideaux sont tirés.

THE RIDICULOUS BODIES OF THE SPIRITS

A procession of more or less honorable people. Some of them smile into emptiness serenely. They are naked. A halo around the head of the first ones who managed to take their places. The littlest ones trailing behind.

They pass between the bending trees. The spirits who have taken refuge behind the stars are looking. Curiosity on all sides. The road lights up.

In the dignified silence, a sweet voice sings and no one laughs. Everyone knows the song.

They are passing by the house of a poet not at home. The rain falling on his piano through the roof sent him away.

Soon there is a boulevard lined with cafes where the crowds are bored. Everyone rises. The procession has grown.

Finally along the rising avenue, the line of people goes off, the last ones seeming tallest. The first ones have already disappeared.

Behind a monument to a forgotten time the sun is rising with separate beams and the shadows of the passersby fade slowly. The curtains are drawn.

ENCORE MARCHER

S'il se soulève quand je passerai près de lui; s'il pleure quand viendra la nuit, s'il ne crie pas? J'aurai cru le voir et ce sera fini.

Plusieurs heures de chemin dans un sentier où l'herbe ne vit plus. J'ai marché bien longtemps et je me suis perdu. Je n'osais plus revenir sur mes pas ni appeler. Et je sentais derrière moi ses yeux qui me cherchaient.

Une faible lumière au loin s'allume entre les arbres. Une fenêtre où je ne pourrai pas frapper. Le feu où l'on refuse de me laisser réchauffer. Et je n'ai même pas le droit de m'arrêter. Un mur en face de moi s'est mis à reculer.

Les cloches sonnent au clocher d'un village lointain et je ne sais que faire de mes mains. Avancer malgré le vent et la nuit qui monte lentement. Je n'ai pas de manteau. Dans l'ombre j'entendais le pas de leurs chevaux.

Où vas-tu me mener? L'auberge où l'on descend est trop loin pour y aller. Les gens s'en vont je ne sais où; je les suivrai. Quand une main d'enfant m'a fait signe de rester. Et seul je suis perdu là devant vous, devant vous tous et je ne peux plus m'en aller.

TO KEEP ON WALKING

If he raises himself when I pass near him; if he weeps when the night comes, if he does not cry out? I shall have thought I saw him and it will all be over.

Many hours of walking in a path where grass grows no longer. I walked quite a while and was lost. I dared not take the same path back or call out. And behind me I felt his eyes looking for me.

A faint glow in the distance lights up between the trees. A window I cannot knock on. The fire where they will not let me warm myself. And I have not even the right to stop. Across from me a wall has started to pull back.

In the steeple tower of a distant village the bells are ringing, and what should I do with my hands? To go forward in spite of the wind and the night slowly coming on. I have no coat. In the shadow, I heard their horses' hoofs.

Where will you lead me? The inn where people stay is too far to reach. The people are going off who knows where; I shall follow them. When a child's hand signaled me to stay. And alone I am lost, there in front of you, in front of all of you, and I cannot go away.

VIEUX PORT

Un pas de plus vers le lac, sur les quais, devant la porte éclairée de la taverne.

Le matelot chante contre le mur, la femme chante. Les bateaux se balancent, les navires tirent un peu plus sur la chaîne. Au dedans il y a les paysages profonds dessinés sur la glace; les nuages sont dans la salle et la chaleur du ciel et le bruit de la mer. Toutes les aventures vagues les écartent. L'eau et la nuit sont dehors qui attendent. Bientôt le moment viendra de sortir. Le port s'allonge, le bras se tend vers un autre climat, tous les cadres sont pleins de souvenirs, les rues qui penchent, les toits qui vont dormir.

Et pourtant tout est toujours debout prêt à partir.

LUMIÈRE

Une petite tache brille entre les paupières qui battent. La chambre est vide et les volets s'ouvrent dans la poussière. C'est le jour qui entre ou quelque souvenir qui fait pleurer tes yeux. Le paysage du mur — l'horizon de derrière — ta mémoire en désordre et le ciel plus près d'eux. Il y a des arbres et des nuages, des têtes qui dépassent et des mains blessées par la lumière. Et puis c'est un rideau qui tombe et qui enveloppe toutes ces formes dans la nuit.

OLD PORT

One more step towards the lake, on the docks, before the tavern's lighted door.

Against the wall, the sailor sings, the woman sings. The boats sway, the ships pull a little harder on their chains. Inside there are deep landscapes etched in the glass: clouds are in the room, and the heat of the sky and the sea's sound. All the vague adventures set them to one side. Water and night wait beyond. Soon will come the moment to go out. The port lengthens, the arm stretches towards another clime, all the frames are full of memories, the streets sloping, the roofs about to sleep.

And yet everything always stands upright ready to leave.

LIGHT

A small spot shines between the eyelids blinking. The room is empty and the shutters open in the dust. The day coming in or some memory sets your eyes to weeping. The landscape of the wall — the horizon behind — your memory in disorder and the sky closer to them. There are trees and clouds, heads protruding and hands wounded by the light. And then a curtain falls and cloaks all these forms in night.

LE MONDE PLATE-FORME

La moitié de tout ce qu'on pouvait voir glissait. Il y avait des danseurs près des phares et des pas de lumière. Tout le monde dormait. D'une masse d'arbres dont on ne distinguait que l'ombre — l'ombre qui marchait en se séparant des feuilles, une aile se dégagea, peu à peu, secouant la lune dans un battement rapide et mou. L'air se tenait tout entier. Le pavé glissant ne supportait plus aucune audace et pourtant c'était en pleine ville, en pleine nuit — le ciel se rattachant à la terre aux maisons du faubourg. Les passants avaient escaladé un autre monde qu'ils regardaient en souriant. Mais on ne savait pas s'ils resteraient plus longtemps là ou s'ils iraient tomber enfin dans l'autre sens de la ruelle.

BLEU PASSÉ

Les mains ouvertes sur la poitrine nue — cette lueur sur le papier déteint, c'est une image. Il y a, derrière, une route qui monte et un arbre qui penche trop, une croix et une autre rangée de branches qui penchent. La pierre des marches s'incline aussi et ce sont des gouttes d'eau qui coulent entre les lignes. La tache qui est au milieu n'est pas une tête — c'est peut-être un trou. Un regard oblique pique le ciel et soutient le trou, la tête. Personne ne parle — personne ne parle d'autrefois. Car plusieurs amis sont là qui se regardent.

THE PLATFORM WORLD

Half of everything to be seen was sliding. Near the beacons, dancers and steps of light. Everyone slept on. From a mass of trees of which only the shadow could be seen walking separate from the leaves, a wing freed itself, little by little, tapping the moon in a gentle rapid beat. The air kept to itself entirely. The slippery pavement tolerated no further audacity and yet it was in the middle of town, in the dead of night — the sky holding to the earth in suburban dwellings. The passersby had scaled another world which they gazed at smiling. But no one knew if they would stay there any longer, or if they were finally going to fall the other way the alley led.

PAST BLUE

The hands open on the bare chest — this gleam on the faded paper, is an image. There is, behind, a street rising and a tree leaning too far over, a cross and another row of branches leaning too far over. The stone of the steps slopes also and drops of water run between the lines. The spot in the center is not a head — perhaps a hole. An oblique look prods the sky and sustains the hole, the head. No one speaks — no one speaks of former times. For many friends are there looking at each other.

LES MOUVEMENTS A L'HORIZON

Les cavaliers se tiennent sur la route et de profil. On ne sait plus quel est leur nombre. Contre la nuit qui ferme le chemin, entre la rivière et le pont une source qui pleure — un arbre qui vous suit. On regarderait la foule qui passe, elle ne vous verrait pas. C'est une véritable armée en marche ou bien un rêve — un fond de tableau sur un nuage. L'enfant pleure ou dort. Il regarde ou rêve. Le ciel est encombré par toutes ces armées. La terre tremble. Les chevaux glissent le long de l'eau. Et le cortège glisse aussi dans cette eau qui efface toutes ces couleurs, toutes ces larmes.

MÉMOIRE D'HOMME

De ses épaules larges, contre l'ombre qui danse sur le mur, il tient la place où les autres têtes passeraient. L'instrument est une guitare dont les notes ne vont pas assez haut. Personne n'entend rien, pourtant ses doigts pincent les cordes; il joue et ses pieds battent sans cesse la mesure. Un œil fermé, l'autre perdu derrière le rideau plissé, quand l'air s'étale et que la foule danse, tout le monde danse, tout le monde crie et enfin deux bras blancs sortis des fumées de sa pipe lui entourent le cou. Dans le fond les danseurs arrêtés regardent le tapis.

MOVEMENTS ON THE HORIZON

The horsemen keep to the road, and in profile. How many they are no one knows any longer. Against the night closing the path, between the river and the bridge a spring weeping, a tree following you. You could look at the crowd passing by without being seen. It's a veritable army marching or else a dream — a backdrop of a painting on a cloud. The child is crying or sleeping. He gazes or dreams. The sky is encumbered by all these armies. The earth shudders. The horses are sliding along the water. And the procession slips by also in this water washing out all these colors, all these tears.

MAN'S MEMORY

With his broad shoulders, against the shadow dancing on the wall, he takes up the space where the other heads would have passed. The instrument is a guitar whose notes do not resound. No one hears anything, yet his fingers pluck the strings; he plays and his feet keep tapping out the beat. One eye closed, the other lost behind the pleated curtain, when the air spreads out and the crowd dances, everyone dances, everyone shouts and finally two white arms issuing from the smoke puffs of his pipe encircle his neck. In the background the dancers, stilled, are gazing at the carpet.

LES MUSICIENS

L'ombre et la rue dans le coin où il se passe quelque chose. Les têtes attroupées écoutent ou regardent. L'œil passe du trottoir à l'instrument qui joue, qui roule, à la voiture qui traverse la nuit. Les lames du bec de gaz tranchent la foule et séparent les mains qui se tendent, tous les regards qui pendent et les bruits au hasard. Le peuple est là et tous à la même heure, au carrefour. Les voix qui se dispersent mènent le mouvement sur la corde qui grince et meurt à tous moments. Puis le signe du ciel, le geste qui ramasse et tout disparaît dans le pan de l'habit, du mur qui se dérobe. Tout glisse et le brouillard enroule les passants, disperse les échos, cache l'homme, le groupe et l'instrument.

AU MOMENT DU BANQUET

Sur les murs de cette salle, où le festin a lieu, les traces de ta vie modeste et fade.

Mais aujourd'hui les paroles sont plus fortes, les gestes sont plus grands, et le bruit plus joyeux.

Les limites de ton cœur s'écartent et peut-être de tous les autres cœurs quelque chose aussi sortira. Mais, sans qu'aucune autre voix s'élève, sans qu'aucun silence tout à coup nous avertisse, les têtes se penchent, les yeux se lèvent et c'est une autre figure dans le cadre que l'on regarde et une autre ligne, du ciel au plafond, qui nous sépare.

THE MUSICIANS

The shadow and the street in whose corner something is happening. The heads, clustered around, listen or look. The eye passes from the sidewalk to the instrument playing, rolling about, to the car traversing the dark. The blades of the gas lamp slice into the crowd, separating the hands outstretched, all the gazes suspended and the chance sounds. The crowd is there, all at once, at the crossroads. The voices dispersing guide the motion along the cord screeching and dying in each moment. Then the sign from the sky. The gathering gesture and everything disappears in a coattail like a snatch of the wall; hiding. Everything is slipping, and fog enfolds the passersby, disperses the echoes, concealing the group, and the instrument.

AT THE MOMENT OF THE BANQUET

Upon the walls of that room, where the feast takes place, the traces of your modest and colorless life.

But today words are stronger, the gestures more sweeping, and the sound more joyous.

The limits of your heart spread open and perhaps from all the other hearts something will also surge. But without any other voice rising, without any silence warning us suddenly, the heads lean over, the eyes are raised and another figure fills the frame observed, another line, from sky to ceiling, comes between us.

ENTRE DEUX CRÉPUSCULES

C'est dans ce carré de ciel plus clair qu'on allumera les étoiles pour le feu d'artifice. Par-dessus la hauteur des arbres — des mouvements de vent, des bruits d'orage — des appels menaçants. C'est l'endroit où l'on ouvre la grille. Les raies se détachent du mur et c'est une ombre oblique sur la route — qui court trop vite. On attend. Près du bois, d'où sort le pavillon, on entend — et ce sont certainement des pas tranquilles — en même temps que s'élève une prière ou, plus loin, un plus joyeux refrain. Puis le jour entre tout à fait, les cœurs se rétablissent. Puisque tout est encore remis au lendemain.

BETWEEN TWO TWILIGHTS

In this brighter square of the sky the stars will be lit for the fireworks. Higher than the treetops, movements of the wind, sounds of storm — calls with a threat to them. It is the place where the grill is opened. The rays free themselves from the wall, an oblique shadow on the road runs too quickly. People wait. Near the woods, where the pavilion protrudes, people hear — and these are certainly tranquil steps — at the same time that a prayer rises, or, further on, a more joyous refrain. Then the day enters completely, hearts right themselves again. Because everything is once again delayed until the next day.

APRÈS-MIDI

Au matin qui se lève derrière le toit, à l'abri du pont, au coin des cyprès qui dépassent le mur, un coq a chanté. Dans le clocher qui déchire l'air de sa pointe brillante les notes sonnent et déjà la rumeur matinale s'élève dans la rue; l'unique rue qui va de la rivière à la montagne en partageant le bois. On cherche quelques autres mots mais les idées sont toujours aussi noires, aussi simples et singulièrement pénibles. Il n'y a guère que les yeux, le plein air, l'herbe et l'eau dans le fond avec, à chaque détour, une source ou une vasque fraîche. Dans le coin de droite la dernière maison avec une tête plus grosse à la fenêtre. Les arbres sont extrêmement vivants et tous ces compagnons familiers longent le mur démoli qui s'écrase dans les épines avec des rires. Au-dessus du ravin la rumeur augmente, s'enfle et si la voiture passe sur la route du haut on ne sait plus si ce sont les fleurs ou les grelots qui tintent. Par le soleil ardent, quand le paysage flambe, le voyageur passe le ruisseau sur un pont très étroit, devant un trou noir où les arbres bordent l'eau qui s'endort l'après-midi. Et, sur le fond de bois tremblant, l'homme immobile.

TOUT DORT

L'arbre du soir, l'abat-jour de la lampe et la clef du repos. Tout tremble quand la porte s'ouvre sans éveiller de bruit. Le rayon blanc traverse la fenêtre et inonde la table. Une main avance à travers l'ombre, le rayon, le papier sur la table. C'est pour prendre la lampe, l'arbre au cercle étendu, l'astre chaud qui s'évade. Un souffle emporte tout, éteint la flamme et pousse le rayon. Il n'y a plus rien devant les yeux que la nuit noire et le mur qui soutient la maison.

AFTERNOON

In the morning rising behind the roof, in the shelter of the bridge, in the corner of cypress trees extending past the wall, a cock has crowed. In the bell tower whose glittering peak splits the air, the notes are sounding and already morning noises rise in the only street: the unique street leading from the river to the mountain and parting the wood. A few other words are sought but the ideas are still just as black, just as simple and oddly painful. Little more than eyes, open air, the grass and the water in the background, with a spring or a cool basin at every turn. In the righthand corner, the last house with a larger head at the window. The trees are intensely vital, and all these familiar companions border on the demolished wall, which crashes laughing into the thorns. Above the ravine the sound increases, swells, and if the car passes on the high road you can no longer tell if the flowers or the bells are ringing. Under the ardent sun, when the landscape flames, the traveler crosses the stream on a very narrow bridge, in front of a black hollow where the trees edge along the water napping in the afternoon. And against the backdrop of quivering wood, the man motionless.

ALL ASLEEP

The evening tree, the lampshade, and the key to rest. Everything trembles when the door opens stirring up no sound. The white beam crosses the window and inundates the table. A hand moves across the shadow, the light beam, the paper on the table. In order to take the lamp, the tree stretched out in the circle, the hot star escaping. A breath whisks all away, quenches the flame, pushes the beam aside. There is nothing more before the eyes but pitch-black night and the wall holding up the house.

TUMULTE

La foule descendait plus vite et en criant. Ils venaient tous du fond, de derrière les arbres, de derrière le bois du cadre, de la maison. Chaque visage blanc avait un regard animé — et sur leurs traces les paroles plus lourdes s'effaçaient. Au bruit qui se fit dans le coin le plus sombre tout s'arrêta, tout le monde s'arrêta, même celui dont les yeux étaient tournés vers la muraille. Et alors, à cause du vent, les fleurs de la tapisserie et des étoffes remuèrent.

COURTE VIE

On va plus loin que la ligne arrêtée un jour au bord du sol. C'est le chemin fantasque qui tourne vers la voûte abritée dans un coin bleu et vert; miracle d'un habit mal fait, mis à l'envers, au dos d'un autre. La tête s'incline trois fois. De loin le genou plie et la main se soulève. Le gant blanc est fané, la feuille se détache. Le vent, comme un cheval emballé, s'abat sur le couchant, couvert d'écume, et le soir s'assombrit. Les voix courent devant et le fleuve sourit, quand les tristes lanternes, le long du quai, s'allument. L'heure pleine est passée sur une autre qui sonne. Les pas des voyageurs courent déjà plus loin. Moi, j'espère toujours que le ciel me pardonne. Mais je suis trop pressé des conseils qu'on me donne pour racheter mon temps.

TUMULT

Shouting, the crowd descended quickly. They all came from the depths, from behind the trees, behind the wooden frame of the house. Each white face looked animated — and following their traces the most substantial words were quieted. At a sound from the darkest corner, everything stopped, everyone stopped, even the one whose eyes were turned toward the wall. And then, the flowers of the tapestry and of the fabrics quivered in the wind.

BRIEF LIFE

Going further than the line stopped one day at the field's edge. It's the odd path turning towards the vault sheltered in a corner blue and green; miracle of a poorly made suit, put on the wrong way round, on the back of another. The head bows thrice. Far off, the knee bends, and the hand is raised, the white glove is faded, the leaf comes off. The wind swoops down upon the west, like a dashing horse flecked with foam, and the evening grows darker. Voices drift ahead and the river smiles, when the sad lanterns along the wharf light up. The hour at its fullest has passed by, over another, resounding. The travelers' steps are already hurrying further along. I am still hoping the heavens will pardon me. But I am too beset with advice given me to redeem my time.

AU BOUT DE LA RUE DES ASTRES

Les lunettes s'inscrivent exactement dans la forme nouvelle du ciel. Les deux figures se rapprocheraient-elles pour regarder? La lune et le soleil attendent en gardant la distance.

Cependant les heures tombent plus lourdes et plus longues qu'autrefois.

Puis, ce sont des paupières qui se ferment, des nuages qui passent.

Et un moment de calme et de repos pour nous qui marchons depuis si longtemps. A un signal donné, une main plus fine, aux ongles rouges, soulève un rideau qui arrêtait le jour. Et l'on voit les rayons qui dorment. L'eau qui flotte sur l'herbe. Le numéro. Et la rue, où ne passe personne, enveloppée dans un grand manteau noir qui, de temps à autre, se déplace.

AT THE END OF THE STREET OF STARS

The spectacles are exactly inscribed in the sky's new form. Would the two figures come nearer to see? The moon and the sun are waiting, keeping their distance.

Meanwhile the hours are falling heavier and longer than ever before.

Then, eyelids are closing, clouds passing.

And a moment of calm and repose for us; we have been walking for so long. At a given signal, a more delicate hand with red fingernails is lifting a curtain which kept out the day, and the light beams are seen sleeping. The water floating on the grass. The number. And the street, where no one passes, wrapped in a large black cloak, from time to time, moves.

QUEL TOURBILLON

En haut du chemin sur l'horizon où le vent tombe déjà, il part sans se retourner ni dire adieu. Derrière les arbres, le village s'endort et les vitres s'allument. Plus loin ce sont des illuminations monstres et des agglomérations dont l'ampleur alourdit son esprit étonné. Il se jette au monde dans des bras inconnus et tourne au bruit nouveau qui hante ses oreilles. On annonce l'exil parmi les orages et les pluies de soleil nocturne de la ville. Des cérémonies trainent pendant des heures devant le jardin en fleurs et la mairie. Mais il faut toujours tenir compte du cadre. Enfin, si quelquefois le temps a réussi, on peut revenir par un chemin tout neuf et un autre paysage. Et c'est un air plus chaud qui va dans la poitrine. D'autres visages aperçus entre les éclaircies. Une autre lumière qui brûle les yeux fait fondre les nuages. Pendant que le calme et le silence renaissent et que tout reprend de justes proportions dans la campagne.

QUAND ON N'EST PAS DE CE MONDE

Il y eut, tout le temps que dura l'orage, quelqu'un qui parla sous le couvert. Autour de la lumière que traçait son doigt sur la nappe on aurait pu voir de grosses lettres noires, en regardant bien. Bientôt ce fut un autre ton. Et la couleur du mur changea. La voix semblait venir de derrière. On ne savait pas si c'était le mur ou le paravent. Les lettres disparurent ou plutôt elles s'étaient réunies et formaient un nom étrange qu'on ne déchiffrait pas.

WHAT A WHIRLWIND

At the rise of the path on the horizon where the wind is already falling, he departs without a backward glance or a farewell. Behind the trees, the village is drifting to sleep and its windows are lighting up. Further on, there are gigantic illuminations and agglomerations whose size weighs heavily on his astonished mind. He hurls himself into the world between unknown arms and turns at the unaccustomed noise haunting his ears. Exile is announced among the storms, and the rains of nightly sun on the town. Ceremonies drag on for hours in front of the flowering garden and the town hall. But the frame must always be considered. Finally, if time has succeeded now and again, an entirely new path of return can be taken in, another landscape. And a warmer air streams into the lungs. Other faces perceived between the clearings. Another light burning the eyes melts the clouds. While calm and silence are reborn and everything takes on its right proportions in the countryside.

WHEN ONE IS NOT OF THIS WORLD

Someone, all the time the storm lasted, was speaking under cover. Around the light his finger traced on the tablecloth, large black letters would have been visible to anyone looking hard. Soon the tone was different. And the color of the wall changed. The voice seemed to come from behind, whether the wall or the screen, no one knew. The letters disappeared or rather they were joined in one, forming a strange and undecipherable name.

LA PAROLE

Si la lumière s'éteint, tu restes seul devant la nuit. Et ce sont tes yeux ouverts qui t'éclairent.

Du jardin, montent des bruits que tu n'écoutes pas. De la rouille des feuilles et des branches, l'eau court jusqu'au matin, et elle change de voix. Et, tout à coup, tu penses au portrait blanc qu'encadre la fenêtre. Mais personne ne passe et ne regarde. Et pas même le vent ne vient troubler les arbres, animer cette immobilité et ce silence où ton esprit blessé se relève et tournoie.

PORT

La longue avenue, le ciel gris et les derniers étages, avec des têtes plus pâles qui montent le long du parapet. La petite maison figure assez bien le cottage. La rue s'enfonce entre les murs profonds et au bout du pont tourne le phare. La jetée arrondit son bras autour de l'eau. La lune avale lentement les étoiles. Et l'écume avec ses rayons.

La sirène des bateaux du fleuve déchire les rideaux devant l'hôtel qui ouvre ses fenêtres et tous les voyageurs attendent le départ. Quelques marins dansent avec les réverbères. On entend la musique dans les rochers du port. Peu après le gouffre se déplace. Et la voile triangulaire avance en déployant le jour.

THE WORD

If the light goes out, you remain alone confronting the dark. And your eyes, open, illuminate your way.

From the garden arise sounds which you do not hear. From the redness of the leaves and the branches, the water runs toward the morning, changing voice. And suddenly you think of the white portrait framed by the window. But no one goes by or even looks. Not even the wind comes troubling the trees, to quicken this immobility and this silence where your wounded spirit lifts and circles.

PORT

The long avenue, the grey sky, and the highest floors, with paler heads rising the length of the parapet. The little house looks rather like a cottage. The street plunges between the deep walls and at bridge end, the lighthouse turns. The jetty rounds its arms about the water. Slowly the moon swallows in its rays the stars and the foam.

The mermaid of the riverboats thrusts apart the curtains across from the hotel, opening its windows; all the travelers await the hour to leave. A few sailors dance about with the gas lights. In the rocks of the port, music is heard. Just afterwards, the abyss moves to the side. And the triangular sail advances, unfolding day.

LE SOMMEIL DU CŒUR

De ses ongles il griffait la paroi dure de cette cage. Il était prisonnier du cauchemar ou de ses ennemis.

On marchait au dehors. Une main qui cherchait la sienne le frôla. Plus fraîche que l'aube sur son front. La fenêtre s'ouvrait au vent trop fort qui roulait sur les toits. C'était encore la nuit.

Et sa poitrine libre respirait un air frais qui changeait le décor. Mais, dans sa mémoire persiste un mauvais souvenir. Et il y a aussi le nom de celui qui était la cause de ce rêve.

FLAMMES

L'eau et la clarté de la lune lui coulaient doucement dans l'œil.

Les derniers passants de la nuit traînaient leur sommeil sur le marbre. La couleur se mêlait au bruit. Du haut de la pente, le roulement des rêves glisse avec des éclairs. Dans un champ dévasté où se perdent des ombres, un cheval saute une haie d'étincelles. Une écharpe nocturne s'accroche aux étriers de ce cavalier bleu. Une foule irréelle s'engouffre sur le trottoir d'en face, au milieu des reflets du mur trempé de pluie que suivent les personnages imaginaires des affiches.

HEART ASLEEP

With his nails he scratched on the hard wall of this cage, a prisoner of the nightmare or of his enemies.

Outside, someone was walking. A hand, seeking his, brushed against him. Cooler than the dawn upon his forehead. The window opened to the wind, rolling over the roofs and too strong. It was still night.

And his chest freely breathed a fresh air altering the surroundings. But in his mind a bad memory lingers. And also the name of the one person provoking this dream.

FLAMES

Water and the moon's clarity flowed gently into his eye.

The night's last passersby dragged their sleep along the marble. The color mingled with the sound. From the top of the slope, the dreams in their rotation slip about and flash. In a devastated field where shadows are lost, a horse jumps a hedge of sparks. A nocturnal scarf catches on the spurs of this blue horseman. An unreal crowd is swallowed up on the opposite sidewalk amid the reflections of the rain-soaked wall along which the imaginary figures of the posters follow with their glances.

ÇA

Les quelques raies qui raccourcissent le mur sont des indications pour la police. Les arbres sont des têtes, ou les têtes des arbres, en tout cas les têtes des arbres me menacent.

Elles courent tout le long du mur et j'ai peur d'arriver à l'endroit où l'on ouvre la grille. Sur la route mon ombre me suit, oblique, et me dit que je cours trop vite. C'est moi qui ai l'air d'un voleur. Enfin, près du petit bois d'où sort le pavillon, je vais crier, je crie mais des pas tranquilles me rassurent. Et quelqu'un vient m'ouvrir. Par la porte j'aperçois des amis qui sont en train de rire.

Peut-être est-il question de moi?

. . . S'ENTRE-BAILLE

Du triangle des trottoirs de la place partent tous les fils et la faux de l'arc-en-ciel, brisée derrière les nuages.

Au milieu celui qui attend, rouge, ne sachant où se mettre.

Tout le monde regarde et c'est au même endroit que le mur découvre sa blessure.

La main qui ferme le volet s'en va, la tête que coupe le rayon ne tombe pas — et il reste cette illusion qui attirait, au même instant, tous les regards vers ce drame qui se jouait, face au couchant, sur la fenêtre.

THAT

The several streaks shortening the wall are indications to the police. The trees are heads, or the heads of trees, in any case, the heads of trees threaten me.

They run the length of the wall and I am afraid of arriving at the place where the grating is opened. On the road my shadow follows me, oblique, and informs me I am running too fast. I am the one who looks like a thief. Finally, near the little wood where the pavilion can be seen, I am about to scream, I scream, but calm steps reassure me. And someone comes to open the door; through it I see some friends laughing.

Perhaps it is about me?

. . . SLIGHTLY OPEN

From the triangle of the sidewalks on the square start all the threads and the rainbow's scythe, broken behind the clouds.

In the center, crimson, he waits, not knowing where to put himself.

Everyone is looking, and just in that place the wall uncovers its wound.

The hand closing the shutter moves away, the head severed by the light beam does not fall — and this illusion remains attracting all the gazes at once towards this drama, played out upon the window, facing the setting sun.

LE PAVÉ DE CRISTAL

A côté, un mouvement léger trouble les murs.

Dans cette chambre bleue, sans porte ni fenêtre, une lampe s'allume nuit et jour.

Sur la table on entend courir les mains — le bruit s'allonge — et le temps passe autour, sans rien changer.

Et maintenant quelqu'un arrive, quelqu'un attend sur le palier.

Celui qui s'arrête et écoute — celui qui vit tout seul dans la chambre à côté.

L'ÉLAN NORMAL

Derrière chaque tête, des notes de clairon, un éclair de lampes électriques.

Les jambes, les bras, les muscles du visage s'agitent et rendent le personnage absolument méconnaissable.

Puis le silence bas, la nuit, la vérité.

Devant chaque tête un masque blanc, un mot pour rire, l'âme immobile.

L'œil s'attarde sur chaque trait, sur la ligne limpide et le corps tout entier.

Le calme froid.

Et, en même temps, sans que personne au monde le leur dise, des mots confus se mettent à sortir.

Les lèvres tremblent.

Tout ce qui peut mentir va arriver.

THE CRYSTAL PAVEMENT

To one side, a slight motion disturbs the walls.

In this blue room without door or window, a lamp is lit night and day.

Over the table, hands are heard running — the sound extends — and time passes about, changing nothing.

And now someone arrives, someone awaits on the landing.

He who stops and listens — who lives all alone in the room to one side.

THE NORMAL IMPULSE

Behind each head, notes of the clarion, flashing of electric lights.

Legs, arms, face muscles twitching until the person cannot be recognized.

Then the low-lying silence, night and truth.

In front of each head a white mask, a wisecrack, the soul unmoving.

The eye lingers over each feature, over the limpid line and the whole body.

Cold calm.

And at the same moment, no one saying them, vague words set forth.

The lips tremble.

Everything which can deceive will come to be.

L'AME ET LE CORPS SUPERPOSÉS

Dans la chambre l'esprit malade et le corps allongé.
La flamme perce.
Le triangle de la lampe s'oriente au plafond selon le sens de la pièce à côté.
Quand tous les désespoirs se mettent en travers, que la route est barrée.
Quand on n'espère plus qu'en la dernière goutte, la dernière heure, la chaîne relevée.
J'observe le triangle d'un œil distrait par la fièvre et par les battements du cœur qui guide le danger.
Sur le mur opposé au côté de la glace — le gouffre noir, gelé où règnent le vide et le silence menaçants, la possibilité de toutes les morsures — m'apparaissent les paysages réjouis et souriants de rayons de soleil, de cloches lumineuses, de cris filant le long, de couleurs détachées de trombes claires sur un ciel trop chargé.
Mais dans l'ovale qui tient le visage tout entier immobile et la mémoire inquiète, trouée, usée par les efforts retenus à jamais — on a précisément la notion du temps qui se remet, de celui qui arrive et la limite de nos mouvements en désordre dans cet espace étroit déjà renouvelé.

SOUL AND BODY SUPERPOSED

In the room the sick spirit and the body stretched out.

The flame pierces.

The lamp's triangle orients itself on the ceiling according to the direction of the next room.

When all the despairs go cross-wise, when the road is blocked.

When there is no more hope except in the last drop, the last hour, the chain lifted.

I observe the triangle with an eye distracted by fever and by the beatings of my heart, a guide to danger itself.

On the wall opposite the mirror — the black abyss, frozen, where menacing emptiness and silence reign, all the mordant possibilities — the pleasant and smiling landscape of sunbeams appear to me, luminous bells, colors detached from bright waterspouts upon a sky too heavy.

But in the oval holding the face immobile, and memory, anxious and torn, worn thin by the efforts forever restrained — one has exactly the notion of time re-establishing itself, of time arriving and the limit of our movements, in disorder within this narrow space already renewed.

EN MARCHANT A COTÉ DE LA MORT

J'ai perdu ce caractère blanc qui dirigeait les toits. L'esprit des toits, les girouettes — et la pointe des doigts.

En même temps nous avons perdu toutes les lignes qui reliaient les étoiles du ciel et le ciel à la terre. Les lignes de métal. Tous les préparatifs sont faits, les oiseaux partent, quittent la terre pour un autre pavé.

Les gardes des courants réguliers sont là, les cavaliers sont là et moi je perds la tête dans ce vent qui entraîne le chemin ouvert et la poussière à travers des pays que l'on ne connaît pas. On voit dans la glace de l'eau les hommes déformés. Je crois qu'ils avancent. Mais le courant inverse les ramène, les plie ou les laisse flotter. Ce ne sont pourtant que des images. Les images des hommes déformées dans un grand courant d'air ou un autre mirage.

Et pas à pas — ils avancent plus près — contre le bord du cadre au dur visage.

WALKING BESIDE DEATH

I have lost this white figure which guided the roofs. The spirits of the roofs, the weathervanes — and the tips of the fingers.

At the same time we have lost all the lines which linked the stars of the sky and sky to earth. The metal lines. All the preparations are done, the birds are taking flight, leaving the earth for another pavement.

The guards of the regular currents are present, and the horsemen, and I lose my head in this wind sweeping the open path and the dust across countries as yet unknown. In the water's mirror deformed men are seen. I think they are coming forward. But the opposing current brings them back, bends them, or lets them float. Yet these are only images. The images of men deformed in a great draught of air or another mirage.

And step by step — they are coming closer — against the edge of the frame with the hard face.

LA TÊTE PLEINE DE BEAUTÉ

Dans l'abîme doré, rouge, glacé, doré, l'abîme où gîte la douleur, les tourbillons roulants entraînent les bouillons de mon sang dans les vases, dans les retours de flammes de mon tronc. La tristesse moirée s'engloutit dans les crevasses tendres du cœur. Il y a des accidents obscurs et compliqués, impossibles à dire. Et il y a pourtant l'esprit de l'ordre, l'esprit régulier, l'esprit commun à tous les désespoirs qui interroge. O toi qui traînes sur la vie, entre les buissons fleuris et pleins d'épines de la vie, parmi les feuilles mortes, les reliefs de triomphes, les appels sans secours, les balayures mordorées, la poudre sèche des espoirs, les braises noircies de la gloire, et les coups de révolte, toi, qui ne voudrais plus désormais aboutir nulle part. Toi, source intarissable de sang. Toi, désastre intense de lueurs qu'aucun jet de source, qu'aucun glacier rafraîchissant ne tentera jamais d'éteindre de sa sève. Toi, lumière. Toi, sinuosité de l'amour enseveli qui se dérobe. Toi, parure des ciels cloués sur les poutres de l'infini. Plafond des idées contradictoires. Vertigineuse pesée des forces ennemies. Chemins mêlés dans le fracas des chevelures. Toi, douceur et haine — horizon ébréché, ligne pure de l'indifférence et de l'oubli. Toi, ce matin, tout seul dans l'ordre, le calme et la révolution universelle. Toi, clou de diamant. Toi, pureté, pivot éblouissant du flux et du reflux de ma pensée dans les lignes du monde.

THE HEAD FILLED WITH BEAUTY

In the gilded abyss, crimson, frozen, gilded, the abyss where sorrow shelters, the twisting whirlwinds entice my boiling blood into the slime, into the tortuous flames of my trunk. Sadness in moiré pattern is swallowed up in the heart's tender crevasses. Obscure and complicated accidents take place, impossible to describe. And nevertheless the spirit of order, the even spirit, the spirit common to all despairs is questioning. Oh, as you walk through life, between the flowering and thorn-filled shrubs of life, among the dead leaves, the outlines of triumph, the helpless appeals, the bronze dust sweepings, the dry powder of hopes, the blackened embers of fame, and the revolt, you would never desire an end anywhere, ever again. You, unquenchable source of blood. You, disaster intense with gleams which no surging spring, no cooling glacier will ever try to extinguish with its sap. You, light. You, sinuosity of buried love, hiding. You, ornament of heavens nailed upon the pilings of the infinite. Ceiling of contradictory ideas. Vertiginous balance of enemy forces. Paths confused in the fray of hair. You, gentleness and hatred — horizon chipped away, pure line of indifference and oblivion. You, this morning, totally alone in order, calm, and universal revolution. You, diamond nail. You, purity, dazzling swivel of the ebb and flow of my thought in the lines of the world.

REFLUX

Quand le sourire éclatant des façades déchire le décor fragile du matin; quand l'horizon est encore plein du sommeil qui s'attarde, les rêves murmurant dans les ruisseaux des haies; quand la nuit rassemble ses haillons pendus aux basses branches, je sors, je me prépare, je suis plus pâle et plus tremblant que cette page où aucun mot du sort n'était encore inscrit. Toute la distance de vous à moi — de la vie qui tressaille à la surface de ma main au sourire mortel de l'amour sur sa fin — chancelle, déchirée. La distance parcourue d'une seul traite sans arrêt, dans les jours sans clarté et les nuits sans sommeil. Et, ce soir, je voudrais, d'un effort surhumain, secouer toute cette épaisseur de rouille — cette rouille affamée qui déforme mon cœur et me ronge les mains. Pourquoi rester si longtemps enseveli sous les décombres des jours et de la nuit, la poussière des ombres. Et pourquoi tant d'amour et pourquoi tant de haine. Un sang léger bouillonne à grandes vagues dans des vases de prix. Il court dans les fleuves du corps, donnant à la santé toutes les illusions de la victoire. Mais le voyageur exténué, ébloui, hypnotisé par les lueurs fascinantes des phares, dort debout, il ne résiste plus aux passes magnétiques de la mort. Ce soir je voudrais dépenser tout l'or de ma mémoire, déposer mes bagages trop lourds. Il n'y a plus devant mes yeux que le ciel nu, les murs de la prison qui enserrait ma tête, les pavés de la rue. Il faut remonter du plus bas de la mine, de la terre épaissie par l'humus du malheur, reprendre l'air dans les recoins les plus obscurs de la poitrine, pousser vers les hauteurs — où la glace étincelle de tous les feux croisés de l'incendie — où la neige ruisselle, le caractère dur, dans les tempêtes sans tendresse de l'égoïsme et les décisions tranchantes de l'esprit.

EBB

When the dazzling smile of facades tears apart morning's fragile setting; when the horizon is still full of lingering sleep, the dreams murmuring in the streams of hedges; when the night picks up its tatters draped on the lowest branches, I go out, I ready myself, I am paler and more trembling than this page, where no fateful word had yet been inscribed. The entire distance from you to me — from life quivering on the surface of my hand to the mortal smile of love coming to an end — hesitates, rent assunder. The distance covered at a single stretch, in the days without brightness and the sleepless nights. And this evening, I should like, with a superhuman effort, to shake off this rusty thickness; this rapacious rust deforms my heart and eats away at my hands. Why stay so long buried under the debris of days and night, the dust of shadows? And why so much love and why so much hatred? A thin blood is roundly boiling within precious vases. It runs in the body's rivers, conferring on health all the illusions of victory. But the exhausted traveler, stunned, hypnotized by the fascinating lighthouse beams, sleeps standing, no longer resisting the magnetic assaults of death. Tonight I should like to spend all the gold of my memory, put down my bags, now too heavy. Before my eyes nothing but the bare sky, the prison walls which once enclosed my head, the cobblestones of the street. I must rise up again from the lowest depths of the mine, from the earth thickened by the rich soil of unhappiness, take air back again into the darkest nooks of my chest, thrusting towards the heights — where the ice glitters with all the cross-fire of flames — where the snow streams in harsh character, through the untender tempests of egoism and the razor-sharp decisions of the mind.

Bibliography

Works by Pierre Reverdy

Au Soleil du plafond. Paris: Tériade, 1955.

Cette émotion appelée poésie: Ecrits sur la poésie. Paris: Flammarion, 1975.

En vrac. Monaco: Editions du Rocher, 1956.

Flaques de verre. Paris: Flammarion, 1972.

La Liberté des mers, Sable mouvant et autres poèmes. Paris: 1978.

Main d'oeuvre: Poèmes, 1913–1949. Paris: Mercure de France, 1964.

Nord-Sud, Self-Defence et autres écrits sur l'art et la poésie (1917–1926). Paris: Flammarion, 1975.

Note éternelle du présent. Edited by Étienne-Alain Hubert. Paris: Flammarion, 1975.

La Peau de l'homme. Paris: Flammarion, 1968.

Plupart du temps. Paris: Flammarion, 1967.

Risques et périls. Paris: Flammarion, 1972.

Sources du vent, précédé de La Balle au bond. Paris: Gallimard, 1971.

Critical Works on Pierre Reverdy in French

Brunner, Peter. *Pierre Reverdy, De la solitude au mystère.* Zurich: Juris Druck and Verlag, 1966.

Caws, Mary Ann. *La Main de Pierre Reverdy.* Geneva: Librairie Droz, 1979.

Jaccottet, Philippe. "L'Oeuvre poétique de Pierre Reverdy." In *L'Entretien des muses.* Paris: Gallimard, 1968.

Mangin, Nicole, ed. *A la rencontre de Pierre Reverdy et ses amis Picasso, Braque, Laurens, Gris, (etc.).* Preface by Jacques Dupin. Saint-Paul-de-Vence: Fondation Maeght, 1970.

Poulet, Georges. "Pierre Reverdy." In *Etudes sur le temps humain.* Paris: Plon, 1964.

Richard, Jean-Pierre. "Pierre Reverdy." In *Onze études sur la poésie moderne.* Paris: Le Seuil, 1964.

Rousselot, Jean and Manoll, Michel. *Pierre Reverdy.* (Poetes d'aujourd'hui, no. 25) Paris: Seghers, 1957.

Saillet, Maurice. "La Nature de Reverdy." In *Sur la route de Narcisse.* Paris: Mercure de France, 1958.

French Periodicals

Du Bouches, André. "Envergure de Reverdy." *Critique* no. 47 (1951).

Chapon, Francois. "Le Mur et la mer." *Derrière le miroir* nos. 135-136 (December 1962-January 1963).

"Hommage à Pierre Reverdy." Special issue of *Entretiens sur les lettres et les arts.* (1961).

"Pierre Reverdy (1889-1960)." Special issue of *Mercure de France.* No. 1181 (1962).

Critical Works on Pierre Reverdy in English

Balakian, Anna. "Pierre Reverdy and the materiomysticism of Our Age." In *Surrealism*. New York: The Noonday Press, 1959.

Greene, Robert. *Six French Poets of Our Time*. Princeton: Princeton University Press, 1979.

Rizzuto, Anthony. *Style and Theme in Reverdy's Les Ardoises du toit*. University: University of Alabama Press, 1971.

Schroeder, Jean. *Pierre Reverdy*. Boston: Twayne Publishers, 1981.

Index to poems

269

English Titles

DATE DUE

GAYLORD   PRINTED IN U.S.A.